C000161544

Lesego Tlha

Coconut Kelz's Guide to Surviving This Shithole

Jonathan Ball Publishers
Johannesburg & Cape Town

I love you

My dearest Helen

Originally published in South Africa in 2019 by
JONATHAN BALL PUBLISHERS
A division of Media24 (Pty) Ltd
PO Box 33977
Jeppestown
2043

ISBN 9781868429882
ebook ISBN 9781868429899

*Every effort has been made to trace the copyright holders and to obtain
their permission for the use of copyright material. The publishers apologise
for any errors or omissions and would be grateful to be notified of any corrections
that should be incorporated in future editions of this book.*

Twitter: www.twitter.com/JonathanBallPub
Facebook: www.facebook.com/JonathanBallPublishers
Blog: http://jonathanball.bookslive.co.za/

Cover by Mr Design
Design and typesetting by Nazli Jacobs
Editing by Angela Voges
Proofreading by Katlego Tapala
Set in Nimrod

Contents

Introduction

There are many things to be proud of as a South African . . . well, that was before 1994. Thanks to all the shit we have inherited as a result of overcompensating for something that was not a big deal in the first place, it's way tougher today. If you ask me, people make way too much of apartheid and all the things that happened before the 'magical' year when the ANC and TarTar (as Nelson Mandela is affectionately known in my circles) came to power.

A quick history lesson about the late, great TarTar Madibs (I say 'late' because he was unfortunately known as someone who would always arrive late for functions. This of course shows that, despite his greatness and his being the best black, he was still, well, black). Nelson was born super long ago at a place in the deep rural areas with lots of hills and greenery. Whenever we were forced to watch documentaries about him, you would see those green hills. Looked a little like Knysna but with shacks and many *sgebengas*.

* * * * * * * * * * * *

sgebengas

black people

(Latin: *negronous*
sgebengas

* * * * * * * * * * * *

Now, '*sgebengas*' is what we Caucasians and Caucasian-adjacent folk call black people. As you've probably guessed, the word is in isiVernac. While I (we) don't speak it, we have anglicised some of their words so they can understand us, because they do not speak good English . . . A few of them do, like the ones I went to school with, but otherwise these key words and phrases are crucial for any kind of communication.

'*Sgebenga*' means 'thief' or 'criminal'. My teacher used to call all the little black kids in class '*sgebenga*'. I did not identify with the word but she kept insisting that it was a term of endearment. I think that was when I first discovered I was transracial.

At the Oyster Box Hotel in Umhlanga there is a cat called Skebenga (slightly different spelling but same sentiment) and the story of this cat is that it used to come into the hotel as a stray and steal food. Skebenga used to come so often that they decided to let him stay and become part of the family. That is how I found my maid, but that is a story for another day.

But I digress. Fun fact about Old Roli: Helen says that if he were still alive today he would have voted for the Democratic Alliance. And I believe everything our Eternal Leader says as she was one of the advisors on the Bible. She also wrote the Constitution with the ink from her eyeliner-stained, beautiful white tears, swam to Robben Island to free Mandela and taught him how to defend himself through the arts of boxing and elocution. It is she who taught him his world-famous dance moves. After all, she is a hip hop dance teacher at the White Power Dance Academy for Colonised Bodies.

But I digress *again*. TarTar went to jail, probably for stealing, but it so happens that he actually learnt from everything that happened to him in jail and changed for the better. He was famous for his rock art – he specialised in limestone quarry rock.

He was a good man – one of the best ones, really – because he had many white friends and made sure that, under his watch, the white genocide would be avoided . . . or at least postponed until now 😊. He is probably most famous for holding FW de Klerk's hand, on TV actually, and making sure we all feel safe at night from the black boogeyman.

However, all his hard work to invent the rainbow nation (there is no black in a rainbow), which at the time might've seemed like a great idea, has actually resulted in one massive shithole. In the words of Urban Dictionary, a shithole is a place that is 'nearly completely devoid of any cultural, economic, or career opportunities'.

Now, we know that policies like black economic empowerment and affirmative action have meant that Caucasians no longer have economic or career opportunities. You probably want to point out that they are still the wealthiest race group and the one with the lowest unemployment rate, but they definitely have fewer cultural, economic or career opportunities than during apartheid. #thinkaboutit

There's a very true saying that goes as follows: 'When you're accustomed to privilege, equality feels like oppression.' Did they ask to be born white? And if you are white, why should you have to suffer for things that happened before you were born? Especially when you don't see colour (except for when you are angry or threatened or just in a place where you are outnumbered or generally every day).

I find the current situation totally unfair. It is oppressive to have policies in place that seek to correct something that was working just fine for white people only. It is reverse racism, actually. It is apartheid but just the other way around – well, without the oppressive laws and stuff. The murder rate is still the same, except that, instead of black kids, it is white farmers who are being killed and that makes it sadder. One to two farmers die every year and it is this genocide that has contributed to the demise of our once-beautiful land.

Currently the only president in the world that makes everything great is Donald Trump. Theresa May was also of the old school and mistrustful of Arab and African *sgebengas*, but it's her successor, Boris Johnson, who will really ensure that Trump doesn't remain alone in his outspokenness.

All African countries and Haiti = shithole countries of the world

The reason I bring Trump up is because he said what we all know to be true . . . of all African countries and of Haiti, too, because Haiti is the Africa of the Caribbean. We are the shithole countries of the world. If the United States of America, with its high number of mass shootings, can look at *us* and say, 'Now that place is shitty,' then we know things are really bad.

For this reason, I have written this survival guide. Because even if you live in a shithole, it does not mean you have to be ... well ... shit.

There is only one way to survive and even thrive in the Third World, and that is by being as Caucasian as you possibly can. Hopefully, you are lucky enough to have been born that way, but if not, the answer is to undergo a Caucasian conversion, like I have, and elevate yourself to whiteness.

Fact: white people have it easier in life because they deserve it. It is a widely known urban legend that white people did something so great in their past lives that they are rewarded with Caucasity in this life.

I therefore offer a guide for how to achieve peak Caucasity that will allow you to survive this shithole.

'Whiteness is next to godliness', or whatever the Bible says. If you act and appear white, you automatically become less of a threat. People stop calling the police to investigate why you are in their neighbourhood, you are told that you speak English well, you get to look at property in Cape Town and, best of all, you get the best jobs for the best black. You will also be invited to the neighbourhood WhatsApp group that will finally give *you* the opportunity to report suspicious black people in your suburb.

The Caucasian conversion can be challenging at times and there are many potholes to look out for on your road to whiteness. You will catch yourself slipping, sometimes, but this is because, as with all transitions, it is a gradual process.

Keep going, because once you reach the other side you will never want to go back.

Let me tell you a little bit about my own journey and why I am qualified to write this guide. I am a democracy baby, meaning I was born in 1994 when TarTar had ascended to power and black privilege. I am part of the first crop of children who were born in freedom. This was also the time when black people needed to start getting over it, because the past is the past.

My slave birth name is Kelello. I know, right – yuck! My friends first started calling me Kelz in primary school because they said out of all the black girls, I was the best and friendliest one and not threatening at all. They said sometimes they even forgot that I was black because I'm not like the others. After being forced to be Scary Spice for so many years, I was finally allowed to be Posh Spice.

It was then that I realised I was special and designed for something more significant in life. It also confirmed what I had known all along – I was born in the wrong skin. A punishment, of course, for something terrible I had done in a previous life.

I first started feeling better than '*uzenza ngcono*' (you think you're better), as my *sisi* (the polite term for your maid – trust me, they love it) says. It was thanks to this daily affirmation from her and others like her that I realised I have a special ability to chameleon in and out of the world of Caucasity. After having spent significant time on the Line of Caucus, I never wanted to leave.

When I first read about American author Rachel Dolezal and her touching story of transracialism (she was born to white parents, but self-identifies as black) I knew I had the same thing (just the other way around). I have spent twenty-one years in white spaces, perfecting the curl of my tongue and 'that smile', which says 'Your blackness makes me uncomfortable, but if I let you see that, you will attack'.

I now feel I have all the required inside information about how to achieve what was once thought of as unattainable.

Apart from my lived experience, I am also an anthropology major at Quota University for Orchestrated Transitional Africans (QUOTA). My advice and guidance therefore have a scientific base. In anthropology, we study and dissect people's way of life and world views, and try to understand human interactions in different social groupings, including families, communities, networks, organisations, societies and nations.

My thesis every year has focused on different aspects of Caucasity. As I am in my final year, I am also submitting this guide as my entry to honours where I will focus on the transracial part of the process. This entails coming out to your parents and finding the right kind of support, as well as the best surgical procedures and medicine to achieve a pink skin and milky blue eyes.

So, now that you know a little bit more about me and my qualifications, let's begin on our journey to Caucasity and surviving this shithole.

Dealing with the other races
(when you really can't avoid them)

There comes a time in every white person's life when, no matter how safe and lily-white you think your spaces are, whether they be restaurants, country clubs, suburbs, etc., you will be confronted with the reality that is living in South Africa – The Others.

You will come to a point where, even though you do your utmost best to find places that are least open to the dreaded integration with other races, you won't be able to avoid them. This unchecked infiltration can even happen at your favourite hangouts.

Now, some interactions are tolerable – for instance, where very few to no words are exchanged and there is obviously no touching. But still, you will have to make horrific small talk where you will have to engage them; worst of all, it will be on an equal footing.

I do not have to tell you how much I yearn for the good old days of apartheid. Of course, I am too young to have experienced it but I have heard my friends' parents talk and reminisce about it and I can't tell you the FOMO (fear of missing out) I experience. They talk proudly of how they used to have separate entrances, bars, parties, transport, beaches and, of course, suburbs.

Nowadays, you'll be lucky if you can eat in peace without being accosted by their very presence in places you trusted to maintain a certain level of Caucasity. I have been to too many places in which my friends assured me we would not have to deal with The Others but there they were, arrogant as can be and not at all appreciative of the fact that we are gracious enough to even allow them in. The attitude is the same as when they speak about the end of apartheid with no gratitude whatsoever to De Klerk and the 1992 referendum on ending apartheid.

In America, they are lucky: The Others are called minorities because they are outnumbered. Same goes for Australia where there's an even bigger gap, which is why it is the most ideal place to emigrate to when you've just about had enough of 'equality'... which is more like reverse racism and a form of white oppression, if you ask me, but anyhoo.

The Others are divided into three different groupings. As an anthropology student, I have studied all three groups and will share my insight and advice on how best to navigate a situation should you ever find yourself having to deal with any of them first hand.

Do not be afraid: carry this guide with you and simply pull it out when needed. You will see how easy it is to get out of sticky situations without getting into trouble or being harmed. Note that this chapter also served as my entrance project to university, so not only is it academically accurate, but my many experiences of getting out of racially tinged predicaments serve as further proof that you cannot do without this guide.

Before I get started, another tip: when encountering a member of one of these groups, I find it useful to talk more slowly than usual and to use the speech affectation specific to the group you are engaging with.

Blacks, also known as Africans (Latin: *Negronous sgebenga*)

This is a proud people. But, like, too proud for their very little achievements, you know? They are usually easy to spot by their broad noses (to smell *shisa nyama* and to sniff out people they could potentially rob).

They feed on a special brand of maize that they call *pap* (imagine a harder polenta) and *nyama*, which is meat. Their watering holes are called shebeens: a tavern (usually illegal – something of a speakeasy) where cheap alcohol is served and drum-heavy music blares throughout the night.

> Broad noses
> (to smell *shisa nyama*)

The hindquarters of the black stand out in an aggressive and arrogant manner. They usually hunt in packs of about eight to ten and are most active at nighttime.

They generally hold the jobs that no one wants but if they just worked harder and stopped blaming everything on the past, they would have got a lot further in life. Also, they can blame the ANC they keep voting for. They are rather emotional when voting, so it is clear they do not want anything to change for them.

They enjoy watching a variety of local programming, including a show called *Isibaya* (which I assume has something to do with the bay) and another called *Generations* which my gogo – erm, sorry, I mean my granny – used to watch. (Side note: every now and then the old you might slip through, like what just happened with me. It is vital not to be too hard on yourself. Apologise to everyone you might have offended with your blackness, forgive yourself and move on.)

A new subspecies has since broken away from the original species. I also come from this new subspecies and, trust me, it is generally much easier to train one of us. However, some have developed an extremely annoying trend called 'wokeness' which makes them even more on edge and vicious with their words than one could imagine.

Some of them will trick you into thinking they are more docile – for instance, they will have smooth hair that will make it seem like they are beginning the transitional phase . . . and they will speak so well. But beware, they are still very much indoctrinated by the past, and think it was all a bad thing. They do not appreciate the opportunity to be allowed to go to some of the best schools in the country. Instead, they gather in crowds and bash the heroes after whom these historic landmark schools were named (👀 Rhodes 👀).

How should you approach them? It is best to go with a peace offering. This can be in the form of pure cash but my gardener told me about something called a 'dumpie of zama-lek' (which I found out is a 500 ml bottle of beer). They seem to go wild, in a good way, at this offering and immediately become your friend, or *chomi* as they say. If you bump into one of the bad blacks, they will take champagne, or 'champopo', for refer-ence, if they ask like that.

Dumpie of zamalek = 500 ml bottle of beer

For some remarkable reason, the woke ones do not enjoy being told that they speak English well. I do not fully understand why. Growing up, and even now, this was by far my favourite compliment. There is no pride greater than a white person assuming, as is fair even in 2019, that you do not speak English and then being pleasantly surprised when you not only speak the language well, but even without an accent.

Do not under any circumstances ask to touch their mane. They become overly hostile. Watch for the telltale signs of attack – they will squint their eyes as if they are trying to see better where the hell you got the audacity to even try. Do not tell them that your natural superiority gave you the confi-dence – this is an invitation for a duel.

Learning to speak an African language is the best way to disarm them, and by 'them' I mean all the blacks. They will even make offerings for you to keep your land when the race war eventually comes. I have not yet unpacked what it is that makes them so excited but trust me, it's a goodie!

Oh, and they love to dance. Boy, Do. They. Love. It! This is actually something all The Others have in common. Once again, if you can learn how to dance, you will have earned yourself lifelong fans who will clap their hands as enthusiastically as we do when our plane lands.

Their voices are big and strong and LOUD. This is not actually a sign of hostility; rather, they use their voices to express joy. It is very distracting in a restaurant and *so* inconsiderate (in fact, they are known for the inconsiderate volumes at which they speak at all times), but this is a battle you will lose if you involve the manager. Just ask for a table furthest away and continue to live your life in peace.

Another phrase that gets them riled up is 'you people'. Please, whatever you do, do not use it. Yes, we all know it is by far the easiest way to refer to a group of them – otherwise, how will they know who is being addressed? But believe me, just find another way. Calling them 'you people' is basically akin to firing off a gun next to an unsuspecting horse.

And lastly, make sure to have all your expensive and prized possessions hidden from sight during any interaction or you will go home *sans* phone/wallet/ring/car! They are a crafty bunch and will use any opportunity to steal or loot, as we have seen with our current government.

Never put your trust in them. Not even the car guard who calls you 'my friend'. That is asking for a betrayal that you will take years to recover from. The kind of betrayal that makes you call them the k-word under your breath, rightfully so.

Indian people (Latin: *And alleus, and alleus*)

Indian people are an incredibly interesting case study. To be able to complete this part of my thesis, I lived in Durban for a while to do research. The intention was to be there for four months but it was too hot, so I only stayed for matric rage. I came across many different variations of this species and consequently had to work and rework my hypothesis and findings.

Indian people
(Latin: *And alleus,
and alleus*)

Just a disclaimer: I have never had Indian friends so the internet is all I had to go on. My professor also never had Indian friends, so even when marking my thesis, he had his own disclaimer. However, as a great student of cultures (because my friends and I need to know what to appropriate), I feel it in my spirit that I'm spot on.

The female of this species is usually spotted by the red dot on her forehead. This dot is a symbol of when they entered South Africa and received their resident tags. I read this on Wikipedia, so I am not 100 per cent sure of its accuracy but as I always say, even a broken watch is right twice a day.

The men use a lot of gel. This is because they need to make their hair spiky as they use it as a weapon in their dance fights. The women usually have long hair. Looong. This is because most of them make money from making wigs and weaves for us who want to blend in.

Both the men and women wear bright outfits called saris. This is so that when they get lost when they are out for, say, a drink or dinner, they can easily find one another. It is also the outfit of choice because it is easiest to dance in in the heat. I told you, The Others are all dancers. Music works on them like a snake charmer! They are known to hypnotise people, so be very careful not to look into their eyes for too long.

They are mostly omnivorous, with some leaning towards a herbivorous diet. This is because they really like cows. Is it similar to how we like puppies and call them our best friends, you may ask. Yeah, it's like that.

They will try to distract you with their aromas and enticing curry. But remember, Indian food is not meant for sensitive palates. Can you believe they use more spices than just regular salt and pepper? That is totally unnecessary and only comes off as extravagant. No one wants to eat overly extravagant food, so just avoid it.

They are perhaps the most expressive of the group. When they talk, it is almost like they are dancing. When you see them speak, the racism that you have fought so hard to disguise will want to jump out. Contain yourself.

Hot tip:
Do not mimic
Indian accents

Never, ever imitate them (and by 'them', I also mean all the groups of The Others), no matter the circumstances. Now, here's a hot tip for avoiding confrontation: do not mimic their accents. That is, do not speak how you think they talk just because you're talking to them. Include gestures and movements under this ban. Just don't do it.

This is a species that likes to travel in big groups. When they are on holiday, you can expect groups of about fifteen to twenty. And that is at the lower end. So, please keep in mind that, if you get into a fight with one of them, there are usually cousins and uncles and aunties not too far away, waiting to help defend their family. Rather choose reconciliation.

Plus, Indians always know someone who can zhoosh up your car and make it super fancy, if you humble yourself. Also, they have the best massage parlours. Oh wait, that is Thai people. Or is it the Japanese? LOLz, something Asian. Whatevs.

Indians are a step above black people. They are easier to reason with but quicker to anger. When they do get angry, perhaps tell a joke about black people. You will both laugh; having found common ground, you will have avoided a fight with negative consequences.

You'll also find a few *sgebengas* among them, but they are rather discreet. They will tell you they have a special price on something that was actually cheaper before you started the conversation. My friend Jenna said this happened to her at Oriental Plaza in Fordsburg. She is so brave to have gone all that way past the Glenhove offramp! She's the one we call Joan of Arc for always winning these battles.

Anyway, I'm getting distracted.

Fortunately, you won't have to deal with them too much. Indians are much more easily avoidable outside of Durban than the black folk. 😖

Coloureds (Latin: *Joumasepoeseous aweh*)

I have limited experience with Coloured people but we did have a few at school. They said they were 'mixed race' but what is the difference? Please.

They are easy to spot: their mane is usually curly and shoulder length – this applies to both males and females.

● ● ● ● ● ● ● ● ● ● ● ● ● ● ●

Coloureds
(Latin:
joumasepoeseous
aweh)

● ● ● ● ● ● ● ● ● ● ● ● ● ● ●

This is a strange species. You want to trust them more because they look more like white people, and speak Afrikaans too, but then you realise they could simply have learnt the language just to get us to trust them before they go into attack mode.

Coloureds will usually be found standing with their hands behind their back as they begin to ask you for various things. If asking for things were a national sport, they'd get first place every time. I think it is a distraction so when you see one, pull your bag in closer, and make sure he sees you do it. He needs to know you are not here to play games and that you are pro-tected. Then lift your finger and shout, '*Jy moenie!*' (pro-nounced 'dzay moenie' – don't ask why, this it just how it is).

Now, how can you tell your Trevor Noah from your every-day 26? Just ask them to say 'chew' really hard and if any teeth move in the front row, you know you have the more dangerous type. But by that point you will be lucky if you have not already been stabbed.

They enjoy laughing, so hopefully you focused in Afrikaans class for long enough to make that happen. And they do not like pretenders. They take offence at that. Although as a Trevor, it is easier to pretend you are Coloured.

You can also spot them by the brands they wear. They love sports brands even though they are not really known for being very sporty – anything from Fila and Kappa to Adidas shell tops.

You do not want to start a fight with these people. They are known for their street-fighting skills and will overpower you in seconds. If it ever gets to this point (through no fault of your own), best is to try to establish a family connection. Grab at any relation or link to you, regardless how weak, and watch the anger subside.

An important thing to know when dealing with the different groupings within The Others is that all of them call female adults 'auntie' and male

● ● ● ● ● ● ● ● ● ● ● ●
'Jy moenie'
pronounced
dzay moenie
● ● ● ● ● ● ● ● ● ● ● ●

adults 'uncle'. I don't know why this is because, unlike the British royals, they are not, in fact, all related.

I suspect they do this because they have so many family members and community members so it becomes difficult to remember all the names. This makes things much easier in these overpopulated communities. Of course, there is a *small* possibility that they actually mean a relative when they say uncle or auntie.

And now for my last bit of advice for how to avoid confrontation and stay on the friendly side of The Others. Make sure that you always practise a fancy and rhythm-positive handshake before you are about to meet any of them. This is a people of 'dancey' introductions and, although this in itself will not cause an altercation, it can be embarrassing to be on the receiving end of a handshake that has turned into a hug you can't pull out of. Anyone can be your teacher, but you obviously want someone who has something to lose by embarrassing you should they teach you the wrong thing.

If you feel a little overwhelmed by all of this, don't stress. While you'll find all the different kinds of The Others overly represented in the big cities, you can always take a break from it all by taking a trip to the dorpies and rural parts. There, you can relax in a white zone where the only black people will be the ones who are working in menial jobs; unlike those ones in Joburg, they know their place!

Let's face it: unfortunately, South Africa is a rainbow nation. Until all of our visas to Australia are processed, we are stuck here with Them. The least you could do is to learn how to communicate effectively: it will then be easier to convey that you mean them no harm, but also that you won't hesitate to call the police should it seem like they are having too much fun or are generally just going about their business in a way that offends you.

Look
the
part

Look
the
part
Look
the
part
Look
the
part

1

Suburbia: How to live your best (white) life

I think we all agree that where you live says a lot about who you are or aspire to be. This is what separates the *blankes* from the *nie-blankes*, the innocents from the *sgebengas*. Picking the right neighbourhood is what takes you closer to your Caucasian goals.

Now, after reading this chapter, you will feel the urge to move to a new suburb right away. I am willing to share my realtor contacts with you. All you need to do is to look at the lists supplied below and decide what kind of person you are, and my contacts will partner you up with the perfect suburb.

The most important pointer I can give – perhaps in this whole book – is: never leave the Greater Sandton area. As my friends and I were taught growing up, nothing good happens south of the Glenhove offramp! People who live in Joburg will be familiar with this saying. If you are from another part of the country, use your imagination or ask a local what it means.

As an aside, shame on you if you are from out of town – except, of course, if you are one of our international friends from the Separate Republic of Cape Town. Now, you guys are super lucky – I hope to get my resident visa soon.

Anyway, back to my original point . . . I never leave the Sandton area. Not under any circumstances, unless I'm going to one of the airports named unnecessarily after a couple of old black people from struggle times, or whatever.

Cape Town
Separate
republic in
South Africa

Before you start the search for your suburb of choice, you first need to identify what kind of Caucasian or Caucasian-adjacent person you want to be. The following guide will describe the different kinds of whites there are, and which region will suit your acquired Caucasian personality best. The only thing to remember is that you will also need to factor in where your church or synagogue of choice is. If you are a member of the LGBTQIA+ community, then discount thinking about this aspect because it's not of any significance . . . you already know where you are ending up.

First, there's the OG kind of white. This is the type of person who comes from generational wealth. The one whose great-great-grandfather went to Hilton and, in 1929, bought a slave and a piece of land for three nickels that is now worth a kajillion rand. That be old-money white.

These are the grand dames/sirs of the milky-hued folk. The ones who had facial surgery even before it became a real practice in South Africa. Yes, the very ones who have a vintage Rolls-Royce because of their long-term affluence, or a new one for the nostalgia for days gone by when pass books were the accessory *du jour*.

They have children and grandchildren who play polo and own polo horses. They vacation every year in locations like Kenton-on-Sea or St Francis Bay, etc. – some or other place where a whole lot of rich South Africans vacation together to heave a collective sigh of relief at the prospect of one month of *sgebenga*-free fun.

In these types of families, no one has a degree but 'hard work' and 'determination' got them to where they are. They have some family business in which they say degrees are not important because they have the required experience anyway, but they will only hire black people who have a master's. Ah yes, the crème de la crème de blancheur.

If this sounds like the type of person you identify with, then you should focus on the following suburbs in Joburg and Cape Town[*]:

Joburg
- Westcliff
- Hyde Park
- Sandhurst
- Inanda
- Houghton

Cape Town
- Bishop's Court
- Constantia

---

[*] No other cities in South Africa apply.

- Hout Bay
- Camps Bay (the few non-holiday homes)

Before I continue, I feel this would be the perfect time to tell you about where I come from. I was born in a manger – my mom had one replicated on the fourth floor of the Radisson 'Inn'. When I was born my parents were senior executives so we lived on the ghetto streets of Bryanston. I say ghetto because so many blacks lived there. To the point that they even had a braai house or *shisa nyama*. The horror!

Anyway, when I was two my parents got focused on the generational old money game and we moved to Sandhurst where we have lived ever since. So when I say I know what I am talking about . . . believe me, my twenty-two years on earth (all of them in Jowies; that's what I call Johannesburg) have made me an expert on the different types of people who live in the different suburbs of the city.

The next subsection of white person is the senior executive. These are your CEOs, CFOs, CMOs. Basically any position that sounds like a type of bacteria. And remember, I am basing my insights on my research as an anthropology student – and, of course, my expert infiltration, assimilation and conversion. I know what I'm talking about.

This group went to private school or a religious school. They all know one another either from school or from work. Their children are married to one another and they have children who go to the same school as they did, or a private school if their parents went to a former model C school (which would have been all right at the time but has since gone to the dogs).

They are in charge of all the banks and insurance companies and all hire one another's children so as not to appear too nepotismy. They believe (and rightly so!) that they worked hard to get to where they are today because their fathers had only one car – and not a German or Italian one – and they basically had nothing because a three-bedroomed house for four people is poverty! They have holiday homes in Clifton and Camps Bay, or somewhere along the Garden Route.

Their wives last worked in the late 1970s before their first child, and for not a day since. However, with the younger set, both partners work. An ever-growing number of the younger generation are divorced now and married to, or in a long-term partnership with, their second wives or partners. This means there are young children and/or new puppies, so the neighbourhood must be family-friendly.

They *love* golf. In an almost unhealthy way. Like when one is sexually attracted to inanimate objects.

To become part of this amazing set, you should be looking at:

Joburg
- Morningside
- Bryanston
- Melrose
- Atholl
- Sandton CBD (for the divorcées)

Cape Town

- Newlands
- Kenilworth
- Llandudno
- Clifton

Durban

- Umhlanga Ridge
- Durban North

We now enter the realm of the urban–rural Caucasian. This is the smallholding type who enjoys a horse ride or two on the weekends. Their children also partake in dressage and they have OG aspirations but they are currently on the senior executive budget.

They live in the city but choose the farm-adjacent lifestyle so that they do not have to be too far from city comforts, but still get to pretend there's prestige in their backyard constantly smelling like compost. They are often dressed in riding gear, regardless of whether or not they will even ride that day. The point is, if they wanted to, they very well could.

They enjoy hosting parties with colonial themes, complete with that familiar tinge of murderous and hostile takeovers . . . ahhh, yesteryear. It is in this environment where the second wife flourishes complete with semi-retired lifestyle but with the money and big house. It's simply perfect.

This is the group where I feel I'd best fit in (if it were not for the fact that I'm more or less in the junior OG grouping).

They do not have black friends and do not have the same awkward white guilt the senior executive has enough of to pretend to care or to lie about. It is exactly this kind of confidence that will keep this property within the family for generations to come.

The neighbourhood for this kind of person needs to reflect the urban cowboy who could, of course, never survive on a real working farm. Fortunately, it's all in the attitude.

Joburg
- Kyalami
- Beaulieu
- Midrand
- Outer Fourways

Cape Town (The Winelands have a similar requirement but different aesthetic)
- Stellenbosch
- Franschhoek

KZN
- Anywhere that's part of the Midlands Meander
- Hillcrest

The children of the above-mentioned group belong to the next group I will be discussing. They can basically be described as the 'I-went-to-private-school-but-I'm-faux-ashamed-so-I-got-these-dreads-during-varsity-to-show-solidarity-to-the-struggle-but-I-live-off-my-trust-fund-now' group.

When they turn twenty-five, there is a ceremony where they cut their dreads ('for like, work, bru') . . . but only on the outside, not on the inside. Even though capitalism is something they are outwardly against (or at least this is what their Facebook pages say), someone has to pay the rent on their overpriced 'arty lofts'. At this point, they become a little bit harder to spot than in the old days when they roamed barefoot, collecting dirt to the point of a black underside.

Although they are not the cleanest, you don't mind visiting them: they have the best apartments since their parents are trying to win them back from the grips of hippie-ism. They fight 'the system' in many unhelpful ways, including only smoking rolled cigarettes instead of those corporate, superior cigarettes. They drink local craft beers, milled by the same black hands they rightfully accuse of being lazy because if they were not, they would have a better job, like them. But that was in 2016. Now it's all about gin. Same exploitation, better taste.

They have black friends but only if the black friends have more white friends and generally hang around white spaces. Otherwise, no thanks. Their relationship status? Polyamorous. Their parents always offend them with their restrictive views on all things from gender to monogamy. Parents are the worst. I mean, we need them for money and stuff, but otherwise, bleh.

They are also not concerned about places of worship as religion is passé and a bad kind of oppressive. Although I do wonder, is knowing the moon's cycle and having a love of burning sage and chanting not part of eastern religion? We will never know.

They enjoy old things. Anything new is phony and needs to be got rid of right away. They are enemies of anything 'mainstream', even if you point out to them that the alternative is the new mainstream. But no need for that headache.

They need to live in close proximity to places that play music that comes from a juke box or vinyl. To them, music is better if you have to fight through scratchy sounds and non-HD to hear it.

Personally, I avoid these types. Anyone who lets their hair grow in its natural colour (gasp!) and insists on showing us their armpit hair and braless boobs needs to stay far away from me. A few scattered vegan eateries around the area they live in improves the probability of a hipster infestation influx. The places you need to be looking at to join these hipsters include:

Joburg

- Craighall
- Parkhurst
- Linden
- Melville
- Maboneng
- Illovo
- Killarney (or anywhere the old residents are starting to drop like flies and their cool vintage lofts are up for sale/rent)

Cape Town
- Woodstock
- Observatory (the safe side)
- City Bowl

Durban
- Morningside
- Ballito
- Kloof

Mixed
friendships ✔
Mixed
relationships ✘

This final category I'm going to talk about is a three-in-one, so to speak, and I've only encountered them in Johannesburg. But if you recognise any of the group characteristics, feel free to localise it at your discretion. This group represents southern Europe's finest and they are to be found in Jowies' East Rand or in the deep south.

As you know, if you want to venture outside of Sandton it will be at your own risk. However, I did make an exception once during a deep and meaningful eight-day relationship at matric rave with a cute Portuguese boy, whose mom was okay with me when she thought we were friends but who almost died when she heard we were dating (I think maybe she thought our ages would be a problem?). She used to say 'Mixed friendships are okay but not mixed relationships'. You see, he's a year older than me, hence the mix.

Anyway, I feel like it is only right that I honour him and his people, as well as their Italian and Greek chinas (not the country). Members of this three-in-one group love to call themselves and each other '*boet*' or 'boych' (a shortened version of 'boytjie'). This can even relate to women although the more common term for them is 'belter', if, like me, they are good looking. Or 'munt' – well, I do not have to explain that.

This group enjoys leisurely activities that mostly revolve around a gym or a salon/spa. They are self-groomers at heart, really, so anywhere with a mirror and a sound system is where you will locate them. They always carry water bottles and even though all the groups of whites I have discussed in this chapter are likely (with reason) to use the k-word, they are by far the most likely to do so.

And this is what I admire most about them – they speak their minds and because they pretty much all own their own businesses and all have dual citizenship with their European home country, any backlash they ever receive is like gel off a *boet*'s back.

They need to live anywhere but in the northern suburbs of Johannesburg because even though they carry much of the same wealth as senior executives, the differences between their recreation of choice are so big that country clubs would be at capacity and then they would have to hire more staff, which means more black people. Yikes!

This group also loves church. But only of the Orthodox variety. Take them near an Anglican church and they dis-engage quickly. This is yet another reason why the angli-cised northern neighbourhoods will not work. To join this group, think:

Joburg

- East Rand
- Glenvista and southern surrounds

Again, while this category only applies to Jowies, Blouberg in Cape Town could be a reference in terms of randomness but perhaps not in terms of ethnicity.

By now you have hopefully identified the Caucasian group you most identify with and have a better sense of the suburb best suited to your aspirations. There are a few other things you might want to consider before buying in your neighbourhood of choice.

1. What are the schools in the area like? If there any schools with 'secondary' in the name, the alarm bells should go off. No place worth its weight in quinoa has a school like that. The absolute best suburbs have a primary or high school named after the area. However, this doesn't mean you would want to enrol your own child there. It only means there will be a good school for the child(ren) of your domestic worker. You'll probably have to look at the nearest private school for your own child.

2. Go to the area at night so you can see the clientele at the local bars. I once made a major mistake and moved to Maboneng. I was told that it was an arty neighbourhood but very quickly it just got dark . . .

3. How far is the nearest township to your gate? A lot of people think, *Oh well, I'll go live in a certain neighbourhood*

because the township is far away. But when you examine a map, you might just realise that your wall shares a wall with the extremely scary and dangerous *sgebenga* types. As we all know, poverty is not aesthetically pleasing. No one needs to see it. Plus, if you live on the outer reaches of Jowies, it becomes a pain to get an Uber.

Speaking of townships, I've decided to add a little guide in case you have an international friend who wants to go take beautiful photos of poor-ness, or if you do not know where to go on 18 July (Mandela Day) for charity work (for your Instagram, of course).

The best and only township for a Caucasian to visit and still leave without an iota of guilt is Soweto. This is because they are so happy despite their circumstances so it relaxes all who see it. Also, the residents are not like squatter-camp poor so again, there's no reason to develop a sense of guilt for something that is the ANC's fault anyway.

Also, Mandela has a house in Soweto so it is super relevant for obtaining the most likes but also because TarTar is one of the last good black okes to have lived.

Now, when you get to Soweto, head directly for Vilakazi Street, where you'll find Mandela and Tutu's houses as well as a number of restaurants (I must warn you, if you venture from here, I cannot help you as I have not seen or heard anything about Soweto's real streets).

Anyway, do not make eye contact with anyone lest they ask

you for money or something else equally inconvenient. I mean, do they have change? No, so just keep moving.

They will offer to dance for you and then coerce you to join. If you didn't move off fast enough and got caught in this trap, just do it. Not only is it a great cardiovascular workout, but the cheers you get will give you the confidence to dance even harder and for even longer than they asked you to. You will have a very short window in which to take photos because by then the *sgebengas* will have cased you and seen what they can steal.

So, do a quick introduction to the township, take a selfie or two with some hungry children (do not feed them or you will never get rid of them) and then head into the braai restaurant of your choice (by now you should know that it's called a *shisa nyama* over there).

A must-see are the Hector Pieterson museum and Mandela House. Now, the former will make you feel so sad but remember, it is not your fault: your parents – and no one you know – voted for the National Party and all of them voted for power sharing in the 1992 whites-only referendum so they should not make you feel guilty about the past.

● ● ● ● ● ● ● ● ● ● ● ● ●
braai
restaurant =
shisa nyama
● ● ● ● ● ● ● ● ● ● ● ● ●

Again, it will tug at your heartstrings, but luckily Mandela House is there to pick you right back up again. The actual house is already proof that, even though they complained and said apartheid was *all* bad, at least they had houses.

On your way out, you will be greeted by happy dancing and singing as you get your sanitiser wipes out and board the bus to take you back to the safety of high walls, electric fencing, security guards and gated communities.

In short, even if you were not lucky enough to be born Caucasian, it does not mean that Caucasity is not something you can set your sights on. Anything is achievable if you put your mind to it. Moving to the right suburb is an important first step, and will give your Caucasian conversion a huge push.

Remember, the wildlife documentarian Walt Disney once said, 'All our dreams can come true, if we have the courage to pursue them.'

2

Beauty tips for the Caucasian woman

There are so many ways to achieve the ~~white~~ right standard of beauty. This encompasses many different facets from outer (the most important) to inner beauty. The latter only matters if you are facially challenged.

Uggos do not win in life. Neither do the blacks. It is just the way it is. So, the less you look like them, the better. Also, having a more urban appearance might seem like the in thing, but it will not get you a seat at the most prestigious and privileged of tables.

So, in this chapter, I outline how to achieve the perfect Aryan beauty standard.

A side note: do not be fooled by what you see in the media. Nowadays, the magazines are so concerned with 'equality' and being politically correct that they put all kinds of women on their covers – women who do not fit what we know is the traditional kind of beauty. You see far too many black faces, with their hairstyles and 'plus sizes' – all in the name of being more 'inclusive' 😒 . I mean, even the white girls are way too racially ambiguous.

Gym

Exercise is a very important part of the Caucasian beauty regime. This is because fatness is a problem of poor and ethnic people, not being able to hire a personal trainer and attend gym twice a day (once at peak hour for Instagram – wear your best matching-but-impractical outfit – and again when the working class is at their jobs to make money). I know, to actually go in and train without their judgemental eyes!

You are going to want to hire a hot trainer. Someone to motivate you, through his sexiness, to become the kind of person he wants to sleep with. You do not actually have to go all the way, but you do not *not* have to go all the way either.

Now, do not think that just because I have mentioned gym, the aim is to sweat. It is not. It is very important that you stick to light cardio: you do not want to have arms that will make your partner feel bad about theirs . . . or that will make them think they are cuddling a *sgebenga*.

A great type of exercise is yoga because the clothing is transferable to the daytime when you are running errands like replacing dying hydrangeas or dropping the kids at school. Step class is also good because it brings balance. It's important to have rhythm – but not too much, as you do not want to be mistaken for someone who has black friends.

The best type of exercise, however, is the stationary bike or a treadmill going at max 4. This is primarily due to the fact that you can still catch up on your tweets, Instagram and general WhatsApp group gossip. Do not let a Virgin or a Planet come between you and finding out that your favourite celebrity has given birth or that your frenemy has finally had her nose fixed!

Diet

Dieting goes hand in hand with going to the gym. It is easy to forget this, but that is exactly what this guide is here for. I am here to help you eat, pray and love, but without actually eating.

Four diets are trending in white circles right now, and it is important that you become one of these kinds of dieters if you ever want to be accepted into the correct circles.

The first (and most popular) one, of course, is veganism. Now, this might make you gasp because in your previous life you were quite intensely involved in meat. This diet, however, separates the haves (melanin) from the wonderful have-nots (melanin).

If you have been keeping up with my videos (if you have not, throw this book away now because it is too late for your transformation) . . . anyway, if you have, you will have learnt by now that the order of importance of God's creatures is as follows: as always it starts with white people; then dogs; rhinos; Indian people; shellfish (except sushi and prawns); Coloured people; wildlife (except the ones we trophy hunt); then sheep and goats; *then* black people.

Animals are *very* important to us white folk . . . This is because animals don't steal and are not difficult to train. They do not ask for 'rights' and they do not strike.

So veganism just makes sense. This is not including the deliciousness that is sushi. And the amazing wildlife we like to wear – I mean, who can resist a sexy mink coat or the incredible snakeskin that is trending in our stores and on the runway? Excluding all of that, however, everything else is in the red zone, also known as the *hayikhona* zone (for those of you who are still in stage 1 of the transformation process).

The most important factor of becoming a vegan is the trademark anger and aggression. It is one thing to say you are a vegan when it's time to eat, but if you do not mention it (and by 'mention' I mean 'shout out') at least three times a day, then you are not really vegan. The nice thing about this diet is that you only have to keep it up in public so that you can make the lives of those around you, specifically those catering for you, as hard as possible. No handouts here!

Order of importance of God's creatures:

* white people
* dogs
* rhinos
* Indian people
* shellfish
* Coloured people
* wildlife
* sheep and goats
* black people

You will not eat shellfish, except sushi and prawns (also oysters) because you need to remind people that you have rich-bitch aspirations. You will not drink cow's milk because, are you a cow? But if there is an amazing cake that just falls into your lap, you may have a cheat day. It is important that you eat this in a cupboard so that people still think you are vegan. When buying said piece of cake, you can use the old adage 'It is for my husband', regardless of whether you have snagged one yet.

I will soon publish a recipe book filled with meats that are not really meats because the most important part of being vegan (other than making sure everyone knows about it) is the game of deception you have to play. After all, you want to proclaim that you are vegan, but without the pain and heartache of never having a burger again.

The second diet is the 'one bite' diet. This is where you can eat anything, just as long as you only have one bite of it. Even better is if you bite but you do not swallow. This diet is all about someone coming to pick up your plate and finding plenty of chewed up food discretely discarded in a serviette (napkin for you, Basics).

Whether it is a chocolate, a burger or even a plate of fries, you may only have one single bite. Then you throw your food away so carelessly that it touches other rubbish, making it inedible. Do not go all bleeding-heart and give your leftovers to the beggar at the robots. It only encourages them not to find a job.

Many people have written off this diet as being unhealthy because who can get full on one bite? But the main thing here is that you need to focus on your end goal – a complete Caucasian transformation, and not appearing greedy like you are a man or straight.

The second-last diet is the 'mmm, that smells *so* good' diet. This is where you go incredibly and almost invasively close to someone else's food – this can be a stranger or someone familiar to you – and place your nose about 3 cm from the plate. Based on your superior sense of smell, you then deduce that the food is delicious.

Note: you will never eat on this diet, but who needs food when you have champagne and a burning desire in your heart? Be careful not to be too convincing, though. You want them to think you are a foodie and can identify the main ingredients or type of food, but again, you do not want people to think you actually eat.

The last diet is the 'pick off his plate' diet. This is especially useful if you are going on a first date or if your boyfriend is white – lucky you! Allow him to order the best things on the menu and tell him you are not hungry (even if you only had a kale shake that morning).

Speaking of shakes, you will need to make and drink one every morning. But be warned – a lot of people have made their shakes but have then forgotten to make an Instastory of the ingredients, process and end result. This means no one will believe that you are a health goddess and no one will take your advice or progress seriously and your special (and hopefully lucrative at this point) social media page will be for nothing.

Food is there as a distraction. It is not to be enjoyed as if you are fond of high blood pressure or Mass Mart shopping.

Make-up routine (you want to be white like a geisha but without the Asianness)

Billions of you have been asking me, 'Kelz, how do I achieve that aesthetically brilliant white-people glow?' Well, it is all in the basics, really.

First, you take a foundation that is two shades lighter than

you are. My favourite colour is White Privilege by MAC-kgoa. I know what you are
thinking . . . 'But Kelz, how can a shade two
tones lighter than me make me look good?'

The answer is simple: you are now join-
ing a world of smoke and mirrors. Yes, in
daylight you will be astounded, nay, down-
right shocked at what you look like. How-
ever, these are the sorts of sacrifices you have to make until
the metamorphosis is complete. Just stick to it, babe. Soon,
everyone will have forgotten your original skin tone.

Once you have the right base, it is time to line the lips.
This might be the true test of how much you want to be a
Caucasian. Kylie Jenner became famous for first over-lining
her lips to make them appear fuller, and then going full-out
on lip injections to make it more permanent. This is why that
family has never resonated with me. In what world is making
yourself appear blacker the gold standard?

If you follow my advice, not only will you have the appearance of a Caucasian lip, but you will suddenly find yourself
saying such things like 'This is barbaric' when commenting
on anything that is deemed too African (black) and also 'I
am not racist, but . . .' will fall very easily out of your under-
lined pout.

Take a lip pencil and, after dividing each lip in half, line
each one properly so that your lips are now half the size. Put
your foundation on the outer parts of your lip so that they
blend into your face. You have now created an amazing illu-

sion. Many women who see you will compliment you on how thin and pursed your lips are.

With these lips, it will appear as if everything around you is too liberal for your liking and people will assume you are either about to complain or call the police. Both actions are part of the wonderful package that you will be able to unlock when you complete your transformation.

If you marry right, there is also a doctor here in Johannesburg who is the only one in the world who is trained in lip diminution (when they take flesh out of your lips to create naturally thin smackers). Look for Dr Whiteguilt online – he belongs to a renowned Swiss family and his surname is not pronounced the way you think it is.

Everything else you can add according to your personal liking. The application of eyebrows, blush, bronzer, etc. are for you to decide on, because once you have the foundation and thin lips right, you are 90 per cent of the way there. The rest, as they say, are mere additions. However, my advice would be to go light on the bronzer; you do not want anyone to think you are of the proletariat or working class. Any job that makes you tan naturally is reserved for the black population.

Plastic surgery

This is a point about which I get into many arguments with people. This is because the world has gone stark raving mad and seems to have decided that black is the new Caucasian. It really is not. This is what separates the Kardashians and their multitude of black husbands from the classier and purer-bred Hiltons.

For centuries, it has been par for the course that white men enjoy a big pair of jugs (sorry to be crass, but it must be said). If you have ever read a *Playboy* or gone to a strip club frequented by white men, you would have seen that the women all have big boobs. Pamela Anderson is a pioneer of this movement and to this day remains an icon of white beauty. She is also vegan, by the way ... For this reason, breast enhancements are still the most popular kind of surgery among Caucasian women aged 18 to 100. I did the studies, so just believe me and do not ask too many questions.

Now, if you are really committed to your Caucasian conversion and want to show that you are next level, you must go for skin bleaching. I have done it. Although you feel like you are on fire for a few months, once the fire goes out and you are whiter, your privilege will know no bounds. Of course, it is easy to go too far and become pink in appearance, but you can just tell people you've been in the sun for a while or that you blush easily.

Another bleaching procedure, which focuses on a different part of the body, is eye bleaching. They say the eyes are the windows to the soul. But if you have dark eyes, you are opening the window to a dead soul to Hades, if you will. Black is all things bad and evil – every Disney movie tells us so. Think black magic, blacklist, blackmail, etc.

The process includes dropping a teaspoon of bleach in your eyes every day for a week until they get milky white and you need to have your eyeballs replaced. Then, you can finally choose from a variety of beautiful colours, from blue and green to hazel. You might not be able to see, but people will see you, and that is what's most important.

Dark eyes = windows to a dead soul

Narrow hips and a flatter bum are also beauty standards. It's crucial to gym these away, stop eating, or – if you are genetically cursed with an African shape – head straight to your favourite surgeon. Once again, Dr Whiteguilt could help, but the main person for this job is Dr Goodold Days. Bums are inherently African and grotesque. I mean, hello! Twerking is all they use bums for and unless Miley Cyrus is doing it, twerking is gross.

Now, black people typically have no leg shape, which makes the next and final surgery by far the most popular. Calf enhancements may be little-known to people outside the community, but a calf is the main body part for showing that you are a person who walks for leisure and not for transport. Ever since Kate Middleton entered Buckingham Palace, this has become the most frequently requested surgery. White men everywhere listed calves as the sexiest body part in the *Maxim* Hot 100 'Things that make us ask a girl out'; calf porn is a fetish most cannot deny. No one ever admired knock knees, or 'kiss kiss' as they say, so corrective surgery to fix this tiny problem (which most urban women have) becomes vital. You will not be able to walk for a year after the surgery, but remember your motto: there's no beauty without pain.

I personally feel attacked when I look at magazines these days. I cannot wait for the so-called big bum revolution (gross!) to come to an end. 'Waif' is the most powerful look and indicates a level of whiteness not many are privy to.

Tanning

Now, when you go on holiday, people will always compliment you for coming back with a tan. Here is another significant point to remember: they only like a slight colourisation, not anything that makes it seem like you are still living your old life.

Tanning also becomes a specific art once you have burned all your melanin off. At this point, you will need to have a spray tan to make you look human again. Remember to choose level 1 because you do not want people thinking you are Coloured. They are a threatening people . . . almost as threatening as black people. So, all you need is something that says, I went on a beach holiday but the beach was in St Tropez, not Uhmshlanga.

Hair

When you Google 'unprofessional hairstyles', the images that come up show many different styles of afros and dread(ful) locks. Think about it: it is scary to white folks when you walk into a school or a professional environment and force your blackness on unsuspecting fellow pupils or colleagues.

Many of you will remember the absolute chaos that erupted at Pretoria Girls' High because of exactly this thing. Some insolent students refused to tame their hair, so the other girls no longer felt safe and could also not see the blackboard up ahead. Anyway, they got their way, which is unfortunate. Tradition and codes of conduct are there for a reason and should be respected. It is at times like this when you think they should really go back to their own schools if they want their afros so badly.

Hair relaxer = prevents blocking anyone's view

Anyway, like those troublesome youths, many of you were unfortunately born with an afro. You cannot help it, but you *can* fix it. Here is how.

You can chemically straighten your hair. This is known as a relaxer in some parts because it makes wild hair literally just relax, you guys. Post-relaxer, you will be able to brush it and stuff.

Also, you will no longer block anyone's view or come across as being too aggressively black. I mean, black pride? What if I said white pride? How would you feel then? I thought so! This treatment does burn your scalp, but would you rather have a healthy scalp or entry into the best country clubs? Think about it.

The second option is the weave. Many women are now wearing wigs as an alternative. But think about this – you are in the throes of lovemaking and suddenly your hair is no longer on your head but where the passion began. And what will you do when you go to sleep – hang it on a lamp-shade? This won't do. Your partner must *always* think it grows out of your head, otherwise he will catch you out and want to leave you.

I hope you have taken notes because this section truly is the most important one. I know I have said this before, but there really is no point in speaking well or going to the right places when you look more like a Kelello than a Kelz.

3

The ~~white~~ right way to get around: Public transport

Yes, I know. Normally you wouldn't utter 'Coconut Kelz' and 'public transport' in the same breath, so it might come as a surprise that I have the inside track on the world of public transport. But I will have you know that over the years I have collected valuable information in the form of anecdotes and horror stories.

Most of these stories come in the form of excuses by my helper as to why she is late for work. LOLz guys, she is never on time.

In fact, she is the true definition of African time but she really knows how to fold my clothes the way I like it and I don't feel like the hassle of finding someone new. Plus, I trust her (well, as much as you can trust a black person from the townships).

I myself have only used two forms of public transport – aeroplanes and the Gautrain. Oh, and I've been on a yacht or two. Initially I wasn't sure whether that counted but then I realised it's actually important to share information about that, too. So I will.

I will begin with the mode I know and love the best. Keeping in mind that this is just a guide, take everything with a pinch of kosher salt and remember to do your own research because South Africa can be a very dangerous place, you guys. You better make the right choice when it comes to public transport.

Yachts

This is the mode of 'public' transport that I feel the safest on and where I feel most like myself. This is because (as you can tell by the quotation marks) it isn't really *public*, public.

The first thing you need to do before getting on any yacht (or cruise ship, if that's the best you can afford), is to make sure you have the correct outfit. You don't want to come across as unfamiliar with the environment by, for instance, *not* wearing nautical stripes.

Many of you might be surprised that this needs to be mentioned at all because, hello, that's why nautical fashion was created. But rather safe than sorry. You're also going to need a sailor's hat or a captain's cap.

When your white or very rich black friends invite you on a yacht, you should stay away from black-and-red clothing and definitely not wear a bandanna. You don't want to look like a pirate. Pirates are the *sgebengas* of the sea! You might need to visit a nautical store (or a costume shop if your budget is set at EFF). There, you can pick up a range of amazing accessories to help make your sail on the seas even more legitimate and fashion-forward. Because, let's be serious, if you're on a yacht, it's for fashion more than for actually going anywhere.

You can also get a monocle and pipe or – my personal favourite – a gold telescope, so you can take a peek at your haters stuck on shore . . . or on a ghetto cruise ship! Soz, not soz.

Outfit – tick! Now you're ready to head out into the open water, as long as you stay in the shade (if you're black) so you don't go darker, because ew.

Remember to charge your phone and buy a power bank because you're definitely going to want to post lots of Insta stories and Snapchats. Your friends will be really jealous and might even like you less. That is the point, though, so keep going.

● ● ● ● ● ● ● ● ● ● ●
Yachting gear:
nautical stripes, a gold telescope and pills
● ● ● ● ● ● ● ● ● ● ●

Don't forget to hashtag things like #howsyourmonday #viewsfromtheoffice. And yes, of course that means that you should go during the week so that it'll be even more cutting. Or just save your posts for Monday if you go on the weekend . . .

If you suffer from motion sickness (like my ghetto mom), make sure you get the correct meds from the pharmacy so you don't embarrass your family or hosts and, worst of all, yourself. You will look like a novice if you get sick because that means you haven't sailed enough to know that you get motion sickness and that you came unprepared. Actually, even if you haven't gone yachting yet, take a few pills just in case the water gets choppy.

Lastly, make friends with the captain and the staff. This is so you can get the best photos at the ship's wheel and hashtag cute and funny things like #ahoymatey – that really gets people LOLing.

Planes

My guide to this mode of transport has three parts because there are three kinds of air travel, duh.

woke = socially aware

1. Private plane (jet)

This is by far the best and most convenient of all types of air travel. And I know it's not accessible for a lot of you – I'm woke, you guys. But my friends will read this and I attract a rich market so it will be useful to them.

If you are travelling private, the best thing you can do for yourself is to get a headscarf and Jackie O sunglasses. Alternatively, a classy JFK . . . but **not** JFK Junior (yikes!). It's totally vintage and evokes a better time when black people weren't allowed on planes. I know what you're thinking – 'then you wouldn't be allowed on planes either' – but guys, if you know me and how white I speak, you know I'd be the Sammy Davis Jr. of any crew.

Oh, also get a square trunk because it's stunning and you won't have to lift it anyway.

Once again, you're definitely going to have to have a fully charged phone and get there early so you can take photos before it gets too full and ratchet. The staff on the ground will also help you with photos. Make sure you get enough shots of yourself approaching, boarding and relaxing in your seat.

With social media being what it is, you always need a banging hashtag. Try #FamilyVaycay or #FlyerThanAG6. The former shows people you are accustomed to this kind of lifestyle and the latter shows you know pop culture references and don't take yourself too seriously.

In the air, don't forget the 'pushing the air hostess cart' snap and most importantly, when you land, post a photo disembarking. And don't forget to greet the city you're in, e.g. #HelloLondon!

2. *Business or first class*

If you don't have access to your own private jet, which is impossible all the time unless you're a Kardashian (you can thank your parents for not exploiting you well enough), that's also okay. If there is anything that will make you forget your disappointment quickly, it's premier travel. Now, this is the VIP treatment all public plane users deserve.

You will check in at different counters so you don't have to be accosted by plebs and the working class. You will then be shown to the lounge. Make sure you go to the specific airline lounge because SLOW Lounge now accepts FNB account holders, even if they aren't in business, so it will be full . . . and black.

You will be ushered to your very comfortable seat. Get ready for a whole range of perks that make the minimum R25 000 difference for international travel worth it. This includes perks like boarding first – because your time is more important. Don't be afraid to push babies and old people out of the way. You're business class, dammit! Also, on arrival you get your bag first, for the same reason as above.

Honestly, though, it's about the metal cutlery versus the plastic stuff you get at the back of the plane. And a hot towel always ensures a warm welcome. In business or first class the seats also become beds, unlike the people who have to stand (?) in economy.

As always, don't forget to snap a shot of your boarding pass encased in your passport with your seat number proudly showing that you take yourself seriously.

3. *Economy*

I don't know anything about this. Just that it's basically the taxi of the sky.

Anyway, now that you're ready for your flight, don't forget to arm doors and cross check!

Gautrain

The best way to get to OR Tambo with as little inconvenience as possible is by getting onto the Gautrain. I mean my dad is friends with Cyril (I can't say which Cyril) and he lets us use the blue-light brigade for airport runs. He's so cool. Such a pity he's ANC, but fortunately he supports a few DA policies and cares about white people getting richer so that's cool.

Now, when you get to the Gautrain, a word of caution: there

are metered cab people outside who want to burn and kill you if you take an Uber. It might seem like I'm exaggerating but one even said 'Hey!' to me. I didn't hear the rest but he wanted me to get into a Cressida so it definitely was an attempted kidnapping. Also, read the newspapers.

To ride the Gautrain, you will have to buy a gold card – they don't have black ones for, like, VIPs, so everything is basically economy. However, it still costs about R150 to get to the airport from Sandton so it's safe, coz there are no poor people on this train. You don't even have to focus coz a black voice will tell you each stop. And it goes straight to Terminal A, which is international, so that's super convenient.

Just a warning: do not eat anything (including chewing gum), drink anything, or even look anyone in the eye while you're on the train. The last point isn't a Gautrain rule but that's how you avoid crime and is just a life hack.

Bus

Now, this section has been compiled completely from anecdotes. Most of it sounds real, but if you want to double check the information, you'll have to get onto a bus yourself.

The last time I took a bus was to my Grade 11 camp . . . I might've taken a Jammie once before I got my car (I turned eighteen in first year) but these experiences were school/ university-related so they don't count.

My helper says the best time to get to the bus is at 4 a.m. I usually take my morning coffee at 6 a.m. so I don't know how it takes two hours to get here, but anyway. And it's best to leave at 6 p.m. after rush-hour traffic. By then the cooking and ironing should be done if she's not lazy that day, otherwise she leaves at 7 p.m.

She has told me that the bus from Joburg to Durban (where her children live) leaves at 8 a.m. and that it takes almost double the time to get to Durban than in a car. I would *die*, LOLz.

Anyway, she was mixing isiZulu and English so that's all I really got from her.

Personally, I think the only bus that is safe to take in Joburg is the Gautrain bus. This is because commuters on the Gautrain busses will have more money than those on average, not-gold busses.

And now onto the mode I know the least about, although I know enough . . .

Taxis

Taxi drivers are the rudest and scariest people on the road. One time, I got cut off and hooted at. The driver threatened me with a sjambok and I cried and called the police . . . He was so big and black. Very dark-skinned, like a real *sgebenga*.

Anyway, this isn't about my trauma. This is about how to catch a ride on these death traps.

My honest advice would be, don't. Have you read the news?! But then again, there's a chance you may be a regular taxi commuter. If so, when you're done reading this book, put it back in madam's desk drawer. *Suka wena!*

The first thing you're definitely going to want to do when

taking a taxi is to learn a black language. I did isiZulu in high school and I know the important phrases like '*hamba lapha!*' (go away!) and '*phoyisa*' (police) and '*no tshontsha*' (don't steal). *Khuluma for Dummies* is a great way to start. Or even *Chicken Soup for the Coconut Soul.*

The next thing is to learn the signs you'll have to make with your hands to hail a taxi. Trust me, you don't want to end up on a taxi to, like, a township or something, so it's important to know that Rosebank is three fingers, Sandton is two fingers facing down and Fourways (if you *really* have to go there) is four fingers.

Taxi hand signals in Jowies

Rosebank:
three fingers
Sandton:
two fingers facing down
Fourways:
four fingers

Go do some shopping, so you can break your R200 notes. This is maybe the most important point and is in two parts.

- You're going to need a new wardrobe to fit into your new surroundings. Mr Price, Jet and even Edgars are the perfect stores for your new disguise. The clothes are really scratchy and if, like me, you're allergic to polyester, then you'll really struggle. It's okay though. Just buy antihistamine cream and you're good to go. Leave your iPhone and Gucci bag at home. This adventure requires you to dress down.

- You need to break your notes into coins. LOL, I know! The last time I had actual coins in my purse was in 2009 but trust me, guys, R185 in change is horrible. And the drivers and passengers are really mean about paying in big notes. I think Capitec doesn't do coins or something.

Anyway, now you're fully disguised and ready to take on the quest into the dark underworld of the real black.

I hope this guide has been truly helpful. I really poured from my endless cup of knowledge, experience and paying attention . . . you are now more than prepared for whatever adventure awaits. Bon voyage!

4

Nab yourself a white prince

(If Meghan Markle can do it, so can you!)

Since we're living in the rainbow nation and a rainbow has many colours (duh), I've decided to write a guide on how best to catch yourself a good-looking white guy. Keep in mind that this guide is for those of us unfortunate enough to have been born black.

Of course, I'm white on the inside, but this is your opportunity to make sure your kids have some white on the outside and will be so much prettier. This will also allow them to marry a white guy one day; hopefully, in a few generations, your great-great-grandchildren will be more white than black. Here's hoping!

If you stick to this guide, you will be able to snag yourself a Jonty or a Dylan in no time. Note: it has to be followed to a tee or it won't work. It will be difficult at times – but if it were easy, everyone would have themselves a vanilla thriller.

1. You definitely want to elongate your vowels

Okay, first things first: you need to work on your accent. Watch some of my videos online and try to emulate my way of speaking so your inflection will be Caucasian perfection (like mine).

If you only speak broken English, throw this book away. I don't have the know-how or experience to deal with that kind of problem.

Black people are notoriously short-vowelled, which is not a good thing. It doesn't elicit trust. We have seen this with the number of black people in jail. Trust me, longer vowels could have saved a lot of them from imprisonment.

A classic example: a black person might say, 'Hello, you guys. I am totally happy to be here.' Do you see? Already we don't trust them because they didn't show that they are happy by elongation. A white person (or you, after following my advice) would say, 'Helloowa, you guuuysa. I'm sooowa happy to be heeerea.'

It might sound like a different language but it's not. Read both out loud and you will understand why most executive positions are filled by white people. It's not about apartheid – that's over. It's the trust created by vowel elongation.

2.   You need to put yourself in white spaces

Instead of going to your usual shebeens this weekend, go to a white bar. Some great examples filled with the very crème de la crème of white men are Jolly Roger and The Colony in Joburg, and Tiger Tiger and Springboks in Cape Town. If you live anywhere else, move to Joburg or Cape Town because what are you doing?

You're going to want to order white spirits as well, because white is right. White people love rum and Coke, so this is your go-to drink to signal to the locals that you have been there before and are comfortable speaking long-vowelled English.

Other black people will stare at you with envy and even call you names like 'coconut' or 'oreo'. Don't be upset, this is a compliment. Don't fall into the black trap (or blap) of thinking that their envy is anything but a sign that you are doing well to cut yourself off from the toxic environment that is blackness.

3. Start doing a few Caucasian sports or get a Caucasian hobby

This is one of the fastest sure-fire ways to catch yourself a white stallion. I know you guys will miss your weekly vosho class or whatever, but trust me, a new hobby is perhaps the most important point in this guide.

A few activities for you to consider:

* Attend a polo match.
* Swimming – learn to do it if you can't. This is crucial, since a lot of holidays will include swimming of some kind and you will get caught out if you don't know how to swim.
* Water sports – try jet skiing, water polo or, if you live in Cape Town, surfing. But only at night so your skin doesn't get darker.
* Squash, tennis or cricket – white people love sports with small balls, except
* Rugby . . . do I really have to say more?

- Birdwatching – this is especially important to them. I'm not sure why, but white people really love birds. Get studying!

Tips to catch a good-looking white guy:

- Elongate your vowels
- Go to a white bar
- Learn to swim
- Go birdwatching
- Demand to speak to the manager
- Shorten your name
- Get a white-girl crew
- Adopt a dog
- Flirt like a white girl
- Get a weave or a wig stat
- Get on white dating apps
- Catfish

4. Hang out at banks and government buildings

This can be any bank or government building (e.g. home affairs or the licensing department). You need to focus specifically on the northern suburbs in Joburg and the southern suburbs or Atlantic seaboard in Cape Town. And again, I'm not mentioning other cities here because, if after reading point 2 you still haven't booked Stuttaford Van Lines and planned your farewell, I assume you're not serious about your Caucasian conversion.

The most sought-after white wives always demand to speak to the manager. *Always.* This can be for a real issue like poor service, or simply because they have the audacity to make you wait in the queue like you're some kind of black or poor person.

What does this teach us? Make yourself heard when you find yourself hanging out at a bank or government building. The louder and more decisive the demand, the more positive attention you'll attract from the unsuspecting pigment-free kings.

5. Shorten your name or get an easy-to-pronounce nickname

My full name is Kelello. I know, right! It's so very difficult to pronounce and terribly black-sounding.

To navigate different white spaces smoothly and really fit in, you're going to have to shorten your name. If you're lucky, and your parents gave you a beautiful name of Caucasian heritage, definitely go with that. If you're stuck with a black name, make a plan. Monosyllabic nicknames are easier to remember, not only for you but also for your new white friends and acquaintances.

So, it doesn't matter whether you've been Zodwa or Lesego your whole life – from here on, you'll be Zo or Lee. Studies show that it makes you seem like less of a threat, and therefore more likely to blend in.

6. Get yourself a white-girl crew

Speaking of friends and acquaintances, get yourself some white girlfriends. Pick them well and pick them pretty because the pretty ones are more likely to have good-looking male friends. At first, and maybe forever, they won't introduce you to them in *that way* because they will not have seen interracial dating in real life. At this point, it becomes important to remind them of the Kardashians and how interracial dating is actually cool.

Eventually, they'll no longer see you as a threat and will allow you to join their gang. In fact, this is the one time (the *only* time) when having a black skin is actually cool. They will call you 'girrrl' and ask you to dance a lot. This can be tiring so it's important to hydrate – remember to keep that rum and Coke close.

When you go out with your new friends, it's time to be on high alert. They will introduce you to the only other black guy they know. This is a trap!

You must ignore him as I'm sure (if he's followed this guide as well) he will ignore you too. Do not even acknowledge him or shake his hand. Any contact and they will matchmake you for the rest of your interactions.

Carefully, and repeatedly, mention that you actually like Jono. Because Jono doesn't see colour, he will ignore you at first, but once you kiss your first white guy, they will start to get it. They might still slip up again and introduce you to Sipho, but remain steadfast in your mission.

NB: when you get into these spaces with your white-girl crew, it's important never to bring up race or any current affairs issues, unless you have spent enough time reading the very important DA manifesto and have attended a few DA rallies. There, you will learn the truth – the country has moved on and there's no point in looking back.

The DA is such an important vehicle to move us into the rainbow nation. Just remember, you no longer care about black people. They are dead to you.

7. Taking up causes that are important to your new friends

Animals, animals, animals! Repeat these words until you get it! Nothing is as important to white people as the helpless animals.

Caring about the rhino and its endangerment was the focal point for last year, but we've since moved on. The SPCA will never go out of style. You need to adopt a dog. Not buy, adopt. If it doesn't come from the SPCA, you will not be taken seriously and trusted.

And if you are affiliated in any way with charities that look after black children, cut ties immediately! They will grow up to be *sgebengas* anyway, so it's better to use your resources for good. They are not helpless, like animals.

It's always vital to research the cause, just in case, but now we are focused on how plastic pollution is affecting the oceans. Whenever you go out to a bar, do not use the straws unless they are made of paper. Here, point 3 can come in handy again. Should your chosen drinking hole only have plastic straws, make a fuss and demand to speak to the manager. Now, the customers pretty much manage Jolly Roger and Tiger Tiger but this will still show your crew that you really care and they will undoubtedly be impressed and trust you even more.

This is also bound to catch the attention of a beau and should get you talking to one.

8. Flirt like a white girl

No one knows white guys like white women. For this reason, you need one or two observational outings before you will be ready to put yourself out there. This should be obvious but you'd be surprised how many people don't go through the effort and then all is in vain when an 'eish' slips out or they call a white man 'bae' 🙄.

White women tilt their heads 45° to the right when they want to express interest in a man. This is important. Tilt it to the left and it will be a sign of attack. Keep it straight and, well done, you have attracted a bro. But keep it at 45° and boom, you'll be asked on a date within a few months. Keep touching his arms, both of them, in a downward stroke. Not too rough, though, or you'll make him think you are familiar with security pat-downs.

And lastly, stroke your hair. A lot. This will remind him of his puppy and, of course, there's nothing a white man loves more than his dog. This will make him replace his love for his dog with his love for you. It's basic psychology.

9. Get a weave or a wig, stat

It is very important that you remove any and all traces of your blackness. One important first step is to get a weave or a wig. Ideally, you should get it in a colour that takes you closest to your Caucasian sisters – blonde or auburn (don't say red, it will only out you).

Stay away from curly varieties or anything that indicates that you have any form of ethnicity in you. A gentle beach wave can also be a fantastic thing in blonde, also because it will show him that you participate in some of those white sports and hobbies I spoke about earlier. When you get to the sleepover stage – and remember, if you follow this guide, exactly that could happen three to six months after reading this book – you will have to get a sew-in.

Don't make the mistake my friend Noz made who relied on her tried-and-tested wig. In the thick of the horizontal tango, her wig simply came off and she had to explain it away while her suitor nervously ushered her out.

He must *never* know that it's not natural hair that grows out of your head. When he feels the tracks, tell him the African skull is ribbed. Even if you walk out of his place in a short auburn wig and return a long blonde, just tell him you dyed your hair and got extensions. White women get those too, so that's okay.

10. Get on white dating apps like JDate or Catch A Meisie

If all else fails, go on white dating apps. JDate, for example, is a dating app for Jewish men . . . Now this is only if you've been following everything exactly as I've laid out and the first few tricks and tips still haven't worked.

For now, start learning Yiddish words like 'kugel', 'chutzpah', 'kvetsch' and 'mazel tov' ('mazels' is also acceptable and in fact may make you seem more legitimate). Jewish men are the most difficult to infiltrate because they always say they only want to marry Jewish women. But once you're in and have made your big, black reveal, it will be too late and they'll be in love.

Yiddish key words:
- kugel
- chutzpah
- kvetsch
- mazel tov

Just ask my boyfriend of two years, Baruch. We're totes in love and he was only angry for, like, a month. He says I can't meet his family or friends or colleagues yet, but hopefully after my conversion is complete, it will simply be a matter of weeks.

If your preference is for Afrikaans men, just change the key words you have to learn.

11. Catfish

You're not going to want to create a profile with your real face or name. This is all part of the dating game. After all, you can't catch a fish with a black worm.

Some really popular names my friends and I have used are Rachelli, Yael and Efrat. Profile pictures are a-plenty online, especially on Instagram, so just choose a favourite and get going. It's better to pick the photo of someone you follow so you can update the page and send some photos as you get to know your new boo.

● ● ● ● ● ● ● ● ● ● ●
catfish =
pretending to
be someone
else online
● ● ● ● ● ● ● ● ● ● ●

I hope you have been making notes as we've worked through each point so that you can determine the best way to navigate the Caucasian dating scene and secure yourself a Great White Hope. If not, just read this chapter over and over again. Even out loud to yourself in the mirror, daily.

Let this guide become your morning affirmations. If you can dream it, you can achieve it!

5

How to hobby your way into
Caucasian circles

As the most trusted and accurate source of information and the source behind most degrees, diplomas and speech quotes, Wikipedia, defines a hobby as 'a regular activity done for enjoyment, typically during one's leisure time. Hobbies include collecting themed items and objects, engaging in creative and artistic pursuits, playing sports, or pursuing other amusements'.

Now, if that is not enlightening, I don't know what is.

While I myself have many hobbies that have become a part of my life since leaving the dark days (literally) of primary school, most black people do not. In fact, they will even proudly tell you, 'I do not hobby,' which is not only grammatically incorrect but it also means that they are usually more into Melville's bars than its koppies (the hiking trails in its hills). But fear not, I am here to help so that you can live your best life and attain that golden membership to Caucus.

This, of course, is not to say that the blacks *never* partake in hobbies – but toyi-toying and cleaning are hardly fun, now are they?

In this chapter, I will take you through the very best of

white hobbies and how you can use them to better yourself but also to entrench yourself firmly in a white community. You will notice that most, if not all, the hobbies require some form of club membership. That speaks to both the exclusivity and the refined classism, with a sprinkling of racism, that keeps most black people out – with the exception of a few good ones, like Cyril Ramaphosa.

A word of warning. No matter what the nerds around you say, collecting shit or preserving shit is *not* a hobby. I am not talking about faecal matter, although if you have this kind of hobby, you might as well be talking about it. So, if you have a basement, an attic, or even a drawer filled with archaic objects that you merely look at and never use, then you are at the bottom of the totem pole and are what my friends and I would call a loser (while holding an 'L' to our foreheads for extra emphasis). I list different kinds of collections below, but even if your item is not on it, keep in mind that if it does not walk or talk and is locked in a light-free room, I'M TALKING ABOUT YOU:

- Postage stamps
- Dolls (porcelain and otherwise)
- Insects
- Coins
- Comic books
- Action figures
- Stones/rocks
- Ships in bottles
- Antiques (if they're just to look at and not sell/use)

There are certain things that make you sad just watching them from afar. It is the same feeling you get from watching shows like *Hoarders*.

Right, let's move on swiftly to hobbies that will not keep you chaste forever. Hobbies that encourage camaraderie and awesomeness. Hobbies that will multiply your white points as much as speaking to the manager does.

Not only will these hobbies earn you points, but they will also help you to find your perfect un-melanated partner to continue doing said hobbies with.

Polo

Polo has been voted Whitest Sport in South Africa by the Caucus Sport Board. Polo is a great sport that is out of reach of regular *sgebengas* because it is also one of the most expensive sports. Expect to learn new horsey lingo and put aside a few thousand to buy the right attire so you can fit right in.

Black people tend to suffer more from dander-related allergies than white people. This is just to put your mind at ease: even though there are polo events that black people invade by the hundreds, it usually only happens twice a year. And anyway, Maps Mapo will be there. Although he is a black, he is also white-friendly – we love him, he speaks so well, he is calm and he has shortened his name so we can all pronounce it. Maps is one of the good ones. He will keep the others calm so that they do not become rowdy, leave their marquees and move towards the polo field.

The safest areas for you to be in during those high-density

moments is honestly at home or in the official team marquees. In the latter, you will find people looking to buy and sell horses and just enjoy the actual game. The dress code for these events is usually derby cocktail chic but, on the quieter days, remember that looking like you're going to see a man about a horse (this is an old English expression – if you don't know it, your conversion is not yet complete) is best.

Even if you have no interest in horses at all, you should find a non-threatening friend and become a member of a horse-related country club – for example, the Inanda Club right in the heart of Sandton. They are not at all liberal with membership, so you know it is safe. It is the perfect place to eat and drink and land a great catch.

Now, if you are a man and are reading this, please note that, if you are not a polo player, you should own a few horses or at least have enough money to constantly have conversations about wanting to get into the game. Otherwise, you are of no value to us as Caucasian and Caucasian-adjacent women.

Skating

Skating can refer to a number of activities and yes, you guessed right, they are all pretty white – which, for me and for many of you, adds to the appeal.

Scientifically speaking, because of their bigger skulls, broad feet and exaggerated bums, black people typically cannot balance on skates of any kind. This is why you will only find a few of us – who are built more Caucastically, who only have white friends and have already chosen an easy-to-pronounce name like Kelz – doing skating. They are also easy to spot because they will have what African people call 'relaxed hair' (they call it this because it is the opposite of their very stressful afros).

Firstly, there is skateboarding. The nice thing about skating is that the names explain so well what you should expect and do. You skate on a board. See? Easy.

Now, when I went to my first skate park, I was unaware that there was an official uniform. The only shoes you may

Balance ✗
- big skulls
- broad feet
- exaggerated bums

wear are DCs – Google it for reference. They are a sight for sore eyes but by gosh do they work. They want to make your micro-aggressions truly pop, which is a useful tool for your transformation.

Then there is rollerblading or skating. This is especially difficult for black people because of their broad feet. Balancing is also tricky for them – once again, because of their build. And rollerblades are pretty expensive (I mean, not for me coz my dad is rich, but for some of you they might be and especially for the less fortunate – black people). This is the perfect activity for getting away from Them.

The last kind of skating is of the on-ice variety. Ice skating is probably the most Caucasian activity on this list. This is because black people are obviously all from Africa and Africa is very hot. 'Scorchers', as we in the community say. It has been scientifically proven that, although black skin used to be an insulator (this is due to generations and generations of black people not having adequate housing, so they had to store heat for the winter), this is no longer the case. These days, they get cold very quickly; thus, you will never see more than one or two of them go anywhere near ice unsolicited. That includes skiing and snowboarding, which should definitely be added to your list of hobbies.

France and Switzerland are the best places to go on a snowy adventure and we know how difficult the European Union makes it for black people to obtain Schengen visas – thank God! LOLz! I mean, they simply do not know how to holiday and leave. They must always stay extra long and have a million babies and take over the workforce and demand things to change to their liking and kill a bunch of native . . . oops, never mind!

Mountain biking

White people love going up mountains and down valleys on bikes. This wonderful activity usually takes you out of Joburg to the dorpie-type places around the major cities.

We all know how those places treat unwanted members of society, so you will be protected. If you have not completed your transformation yet, go with a white friend so she can explain to them that you are one of the good ones and that you are well on your way.

Mountain biking is fun because black people actually do not cycle – except gardeners, who use it as transport, which is not the same as mountain or trail biking. Mountain bikes are very expensive and the BEE types who could afford it have big bellies and would rather be at Taboo flirting with their daughters' friends. White people prefer to do this at house parties, which is much classier.

Hiking

This activity can also be found on the outskirts of democracy and racial integration. Like the other hobbies, hiking is good for cardiovascular strength and perfecting imperialist thoughts. Ahhh, the great outdoors.

Hiking is actually how the Anglo-Zulu War began. Once the British soldiers got to the top of some mountains in Zululand, and they saw how lush and beautiful the land was, they realised that the Zulus would ruin it because what do they know about farming?

Anyway, since that time, hiking has remained the traditional way to get away from it all and cultivate those wonderful thoughts of superiority that make you a Great White.

Swimming

If you went to a school like mine, you will know that half of Them do not know how to swim and the other half refuse to because, unlike you and me, their hair does not take well to chlorine. No, not in the fun 'it turns green' way . . . but in the sad, afro-puff way. Google it to see exactly how messy, unprofessional, and untamed for classrooms and boardrooms alike, the afro puff is.

Swimming costumes are also designed with beautiful, flatter bums in mind. The best and most exclusive invention in the swimming pool is swimming caps. I used to have such a laugh watching some of the black girls trying to fit their wild and crazy hair into the caps. That is probably 99 per cent of the reason they do not swim. Thank you, Speedo.

Swimming caps are for black girls with wild crazy hair

All other water sports fall into this category, too. Anything with the likelihood of your being submerged – scuba diving, jet skiing, snorkelling, water polo and surfing – are great options. Because of the high threat of Them falling in, it is unlikely that you'll be accosted by blackness out on our lakes or in the ocean. Unless you're on a cruise ship. Stay away from those. I have tried more than once and every time it is like the *Amistad* is bringing them back.

The small-ball sports – tennis, squash, hockey

All these sports are very good because, as in the bedroom, scoring with small balls is something we hold in high esteem. Imagine the grossness of a big ball, like in soccer. Just as an aside, if you are European (and only then!), soccer, or football, is still a totally acceptable hobby. (But, like, you-still-have-the-accent European. Not Bedfordview European.)

It is a fabulous not-so-secret that small-ball sports are the hobbies or sports that stay within our circles. Obviously, every activity will have infiltrators, but because country clubs are usually word-of-mouth memberships and a current member has to nominate you, they are reminiscent of the wonderful pre-1994 era, before the dreaded quotas and before everyone got so sensitive.

Rugby

Speaking of the q-word . . . Things are extremely shaky right now with ol' Siya Kolisi being given the captaincy 😵. Thanks a lot, ANC! And yes, he is one of the best rugby players, if not *the* best rugby player, right now, but if he is on the team it is because of quotas. But do not quote me (LOL, get it?).

But yes, that's just how it works. Soz. Anyway, rugby is still very much a proud Afrikaner sport. I mean, it's '*Hier kom die Bokke*' not '*Woza laphar, wena* silly *Bokke*'. The first time I heard the k-word was at a rugby match in Pretoria, and years later again at a varsity game in Stellenbosch. I was quite glad to see very little has changed in rugby, despite the rest of the country being so into transformation. Yuck.

Birdwatching (and reporting suspicious activity)

This ranks number one in *Camps Bay Magazine*'s list of most fun and most . . . ummm . . . *exclusive* activity by all who were polled. Birdwatching might be painfully boring, but it is particularly fascinating because, if you are a person who likes watching your neighbourhood for suspicious activity, imagine how much fun you will have when you take a break and turn your attention skywards.

Black people don't even have a word for 'sparrow' or 'kingfisher': they just point and say '*inyoni*', which shows you how very little interest they could ever take in this hobby. This is also the frontrunner nominee for least likely to ever get peak black interest, so it is also the safest activity one can do.

Reporting suspicious activity, which is directly related to birdwatching, has taken the world by storm. Social media has grown it from strength to strength and, even though I'm a relative newbie, I've become obsessed with it. Now, it does not matter if the activity is actually suspicious or not, or even if you can properly see what it is you are reporting on. What matters is how you feel about it and that you want the perpetrators to be removed from your area.

Sometimes you will have to go out of your way to other areas to practise reporting suspicious activity. This is when you know you have truly reached peak Caucasity. The usual uniform is sunglasses, an unattractive haircut (you do not want to draw the wrong kind of attention in these parts) and, of course, the famous white scowl.

The white scowl was first invented in 1788 by brave colonisers who were reporting suspicious activity when they first rightfully bought the land through violent means. Legend has it that, although the natives were not doing anything, they just seemed suspicious. If you have ever seen an unidentified black man who dares to walk through a suburb without first identifying himself with a board around his neck, then you'll know exactly what I am talking about.

This hobby is especially great because it can be done in every suburban neighbourhood and there is a proliferation of related Facebook and WhatsApp groups, so you never have to play alone. You will need good vision, a disdain for blackness and a smartphone to capture black people having the audacity to be in our neighbourhoods (except if they work for you). Oh, and you will need a loose command of fanagalo so you can ask them what they want or to report them to your security guard.

Requirements for bird-watching:
- good vision
- a disdain for blackness
- a smartphone

Yoga

This is a highly underrated hobby. If you are lucky, you'll have met your blonde Prince Charming (mine is still coming) who has swept you off your feet and allowed you to stop working to really focus on your yoga, even though you have no intention of ever going to the Far East because you are vegan and you don't know what they really put in their food but you've heard horror stories.

Yoga makes you more flexible, but only physically. Don't worry, you will never become flexible in your views. Haha, almost scared the wits out of you there, didn't I?

Yoga is also great for your posture since you'll be spending a lot of time looking down on people. You learn great poses such as 'the eye roll', the 'lock your car doors without the black man seeing you' and, my personal favourite (because it was hard to perfect but once I got it, I was ready to be inducted), the 'looking for the manager' pose which requires focus in both the body and face.

Now, the last hobby on my list is going to seem confusing

because it is so similar to something The Others partake in and use in combat, but don't worry, our tools are smaller.

I'm talking about darts, of course.

Darts

Most people ask me, 'Kelz, is darts not similar to the spear-throwing they enjoy?' The simple answer is no. The spear is longer and requires a human or animal target – barbarism – and darts is a refined English sport for when we are super drunk and think it's fun to throw a tiny spear around Jolly Cool.

Darts is a special kind of hobby because it would seem to be on the edge of danger but it is, in fact, only as dangerous as pronouncing the word 'Xhosa'. Cane and Crème Soda is the official drink of the National Darts Association of South Africa and our national team plays Johnny Clegg's 'Impi' before every game to really get into the spirit of the Zulu (you have to admit, they can aim, hey). Of course, the team is still all-white.

Feel free to tweet me if you are unsure whether an activity will hinder or help your Caucasian conversion. This goes for all the hobbies listed, and even those that are not. I am happy to advise.

Remember, you should always call ahead when booking your activities so you can make sure you do not end up somewhere on what is meant to be their 'urban night'. Otherwise, happy trails and see you on the other side.

6

Cultural practices and
other nightmares

In the life of a transracial person, there will always be a moment when he or she will be forced to endure the other side of his or her identity. Even though you have left your old (black) life behind, it's a bit more difficult throwing your family away, because you need them for inheritance and things.

If you do not come from a family who has made a lot of money despite their melanin, you should delete your family completely from your life. Yes, I'm talking to those of you who have to pay so-called black tax to support your family – start your Caucasian conversion NOW. (I only learnt about black tax when Mmusi put on his election face and promised to eradicate it . . .)

Black tax is when the world fines you for being black and taking up space in the country. It is usually paid by black people who, thanks to affirmative action, get high-paying jobs but are still stuck with poor relations.

I, for one, have family that still live in the *lalis* (traditional homesteads in the black rural areas of South Africa), even though they are distant family. To make my immediate family happy and keep me in the will, I sometimes have to go and make nice with the distant family. Take note: if this happens more than twice a year, you have to evaluate how much you stand to gain from the will and whether it's all worthwhile.

Oh my God, my family in the *lalis* is so ghetto. To my friends I say that I am going on an anthropology course field trip because they will most definitely disown me (and you, dear reader) if they find out that I actually associate with my black family.

I will break this part of the guide down into subsections, because since I started studying at Quota University I have realised that it is easier to explain things that might be deemed offensive if you break them down step by step and disarm them in this way.

(I have not included this chapter in the version that will be sold at Caucasian bookshops because they cannot know this secret shame. Rather, they remain unaware that, even though we aim to transition fully on the outside, there is one part of us that we simply cannot escape. So, read on and write your notes in invisible ink so that, if they see your copy, you can always claim ignorance and charge off to the Hyde Park bookshop to insist on one of the 'proper' copies. Keep up the act, dolls.)

1. Language

The first thing you will notice when you are dragged kicking and screaming back to a *lali* or township setting is that the language is different. This begins before you even reach vernacular differences.

They will attempt to speak English to appease us coconuts, but it will be hard to understand, so keep your wits about you and focus at all times. For example, they might ask you to chop an onion. Now, 'uhn-yin' is how we pronounce it, but they call it 'on-nyon' or 'on-your-knees'.

When in doubt, sound it out slowly in your head and try look for clues as to what the hell they are talking about. Are they holding a sharp knife and have just barely begun to cook? Did they perhaps point to what they need? Is there a chopping board, but nothing has been cut up yet? And remember, an onion is the first thing Africans use when making their spicy food.

● ● ● ● ● ● ● ● ● ● ● ●
Onion
uhn-yin
(pronounced
on-nyon or
on-your-knees)
● ● ● ● ● ● ● ● ● ● ● ●

But this is just the tip of the iceberg. The words that will really confuse you (and this is true of any tribe you might be trying to escape from) are 'bed', 'bird' and 'bad'. When one of your relatives says any of these, they all sound like the same word. Even if your parents have made it out the 'hood, as they affectionately call it, they too might occasionally embarrass you with one of these special treats. For example, the sentence 'The bad bird shat on the bed' might sound like 'The bed bed shat on the bed'.

You will spend a lot of time looking at your surroundings making the best possible assumption about what is being said. If you are outside, always assume it is about birds. Someone acting up? They are being bad. And you are in a house talking about where someone will be sleeping? Bed.

However, if someone is relaying a story and you have no context, just smile and try to correct them where you can. My mom does not like it when I correct her, but it has to be done, otherwise she could embarrass me while trying to tell Nicky and Kylie about the 'bed' that was flying.

Now, there are actual, real, language barriers to contend with. These will do your head in. Sometimes, the better families will speak English – not only to accommodate you, but to improve their own lives. There are times, though, when they simply fail to find the words and revert to their native languages. This may also happen when they are gossiping about you, so stay alert because they love that.

They always talk about the most beautiful and successful members of the family. Most of the time, it is to make themselves feel better about not having worked as hard as you to fit into a better life, but sometimes (and this is very rare) it is just because they do not like how you are. We call these people haters. They are simply Jealous Juliuses – the name comes from Julius Malema, who is jealous of everyone whiter than him, and that is why he sings about the boer (who puts food on our tables, by the way – well, his workers do, but with his guidance, of course).

There is a school I will be opening in 2022 called the Academy for Left-out Coconuts. It will have amazing first-time courses like:

- How to Translate the Bad Words 101
- Are They Gossiping about Me? (This is a second-year elective.)

And what will probably be the most popular course:

* Synonyms for Coconuts (including 'cheese girl', 'oreo', '*mlungu*', etc.).

I will be offering short courses to madams who want to find out what their helpers are saying about them and a translation course for farmers who want to translate intel to find out whether the workers are planning a genocide.

2. Food

When visiting the family, you will be offered all kinds of things that do not agree with a sensitive tummy. I mean, you cannot eat sushi all year and think your stomach will agree with sheep intestines.

They really know how to use the whole animal, probably because they had to learn to make it last because meat is expensive. But I notice that even the ones who have made it in life now yearn for that shitbag of a meal. Even Tashas, once, was part of a horrible and almost franchise-ending hoax in which they said they were offering Mogodu Mondays (big-time gag as I wrote that).

You should pack a whole week's worth of noodles and nonperishable items because once something goes into the fridge, it is *hamba kahle* (farewell) to your food. They are a scavenging people, as thrifty as they are shifty, so keep your food in a hidden compartment and only eat once everyone has gone to sleep (presumably on grass mats, or whatever).

They also love sour milk: literally, milk that has just gone off. Again, very resourceful. If they just used their resourceful-ness in an actual helpful way, they could find themselves in better positions financially. But alas, the hunter-gatherer in them always comes out on top, while we sort out the economy.

They drink the milk, they put it on stale bread and some-times even *phuthu*, which is like unrefined polenta and gross. So, if you see something with a milky consistency, stay away.

They rarely eat with utensils so this is something you may also have to take along. They are a hand-to-mouth people, which is why they have a broader palm and inverted finger pads for scooping the food up. Through evolution, our hands have lost these, because we eat with a fork and knife. To be totally honest, I had to have scoop surgery to remove the little spoon dents in my fingers, but I will *not* speak about that.

3. Helping out/chores

The most frustrating part about going to visit your family back at their Bantu homesteads is that they do not under-stand that you have a higher station in life than them and that your softer hands are not meant for manual labour. I only cut onions once a year and, trust me, the tears are more from my intense sadness then from the burn of the onions.

They will wake you up at dawn, like you're just the same as any other random cousin, and divide the chores. I have learnt a secret that has saved me sometimes when 'ain't no-body got time for that' (as my grandmother says – well, I don't know if that is exactly what she is saying, but I assume so). The secret is to act completely incompetent and cry all the time. This will leave them with no other choice than to come complete the task while you look for the best places to take Prada-in-the-township selfies, also known as rich-bitch-poverty-chic photos.

Your parents should have used some of their money to improve the lives of their parents (your grandparents) so there should be no real torture methods like going to fetch your own water. And remember, the oblong shape of the Caucasian head does not allow that huge, heavy bucket to balance on it.

Sometimes, when they ask me to do something, I just act like I do not understand. Usually they just mutter something under their breath and walk away. This is a victory.

Last year I got clever and I took *sisi* with me to take over my chores. She did not get to see her kids for Christmas but trust me, she was happy for the extra R50 for that week.

4. Greetings

One thing I forgot to add to the language section is how loudly they communicate. So, not only are they mostly wrong in their pronunciation, but they are also loud and obnoxious about it. They will shout the most unnecessary things.

They are also a people for whom phones are still a new technology. Communicating was mostly done over a fence; often, these fences were several metres apart. They laugh loudly, talk loudly, cry loudly and sing struggle songs loudly. Honestly, it can be quite invasive (#IStandWithBelindaBozzoli).

I have read studies by learned anthropologists who have said that, even though black people's ears are larger in appearance, their eardrums are smaller and shaped like bongo drums, so they are only used to loud reverberating sounds. This is also why a lot, if not all, of their music is heavily percussion-laden.

Now, when they come to greet you, regardless of their relationship with or feelings towards you, you will always be greeted suuuper loudly. They also do not know the meaning of personal space. A good place to witness this is in a queue. You could basically identify what they had for lunch and if they are a grower or shower or whether they are recently *Inxeba*'d by how close they stand to you.

They insist on kisses. Goodness me, they love to kiss. Talk about being hyper-expressive in all the wrong ways. The older they are, the more likely they are to trap you into a kiss. The ritual is to lick the lips and hold your face until they plant the kiss (if you can even call it that).

Kissing your dog, perfectly normal and acceptable. Kissing a black – by Arthur's sword, that is traumatising. They hug, they hold, they kiss. More evidence of this people's obsession with smashing human boundaries.

5. Traditional garb

If you are an adult, even in the transracial community, it is highly unlikely that you would never have been exposed to traditional garb (short for garbage in this case, quite frankly). There are many different items of clothing so it is best to find out which tribe the savage members of your family come from to be better prepared for what you will have to deal with.

I, for example, am the child of people who identify as Sotho. I identify as British myself, but that is part of the lonely journey of transracialism. This is why it is important for me to speak about my struggles so much – to give hope to any little black kid who looks in the mirror and does not like what he or she sees, so that he or she, too, can believe in and achieve whiteness.

The people in my family are always wearing what is called *Seshoeshoe* cloth. I can't describe it, but it is by no means pretty. Just Google it. And they make everything with this tribal cloth. Even nice dresses. So yeah, they ruin everything.

All cultures in Africa wear *doeks* (head wraps). Some wear them with their traditional clothing; others even extend wearing them to when they sleep. I think this is because their wigs fall off. It's hilarious. *Doeks* are the burkas of black people – oppressive and out of touch with modernity – but black people wear them because they think they have made the choice.

If it comes to that, rather take the cloth to your designer and get them to make European clothing, so you are not *that* put out. They only do this for weddings and funerals so you should be good because those events can be avoided, at best, and tolerated with a sulky face, at worst.

6. Weddings and funerals

Not a week goes by in which these ones are not preparing for some sort of burial or overpopulation ritual. There are also so many members of each family due to said overpopulation, so you could potentially be going to a 'celebration' (read: clusterfuck) every single week, if you are not careful. If I had my way, theirs would be a one-in-one-out policy so that their numbers stabilise, because they breed like rabbits.

Unlike in the Caucasian communities, both funerals and weddings are huge deals. Unlike the sophisticated, neat soirees and mourning tributes of the members of Caucus, these events are big and encompass many different smaller events. This is more the case for weddings than funerals. Once, I was forced to attend a cousin's wedding because I accidentally RSVP'd in the affirmative – another reason to get your isiVernac up. She had, like, six different ceremonies all leading up to the wedding and at that point even I was, like, is he polygamous because no one couple should have this many weddings.

They do not have much money for instruments or for translations so they will sing a lot using bibles as their drums and you will be totally lost and forced to #whitesmile through the pain. They sing allll the time. You would think the songs would be nice like 'Amazing Grace' or 'Shake It Off', but they are aggressive and long and there isn't even a rap for relief.

Anyway, some of these things will make you just want to pack it all up and emancipate yourself. But again, it's important to stick it out if, like me, you have parents who are friends, economically speaking, with Cyril.

There are some cultural practices I have not even been able to mention because, unlike the directors of *that* movie,

I do not want a whole lot of Xhosa men marching to my house demanding a retraction. But yes . . .

7. Coming of age

These are the practices that really separate the coconut from the other nuts. This is not a circumcision joke, by the way. There are ones for girls and boys. Depending on how long you need to be away for to fulfil the criteria of becoming a man or woman, you will need to formulate a big lie at school as to why you had to go away.

These rituals are known in some circles as going to the mountain, so why not say that your family has a cabin and that your parents just wanted some time away with the family? I mean, they do it when they go on holiday a week before school closes or whatever. You could also just say your cousin is getting married so, even though you are not close to your family, you roll your eyes and say you have to go.

Make sure to take the time to heal, also emotionally, from being surrounded by that much culture, tradition and foreign languages. Your friends must not see any sign that you are a part of such a tradition.

These practices should be denounced vehemently whenever the topic comes up. Simple phrases like the following will ensure that you retain your Caucasity and the acceptance of the group:

'It's just so outdated.'
'That is totally unacceptable.'
'My family is very westernised.'

Rule 1:

Never get
involved in the
slaughtering of
an animal

The number one rule in all of this is that you must never, ever get involved in the slaughtering of an animal. I mean, it's not like you are vegan but when Woolies kills the animal, it's meat. When black people do it, it's barbaric and you cannot get involved.

Once you have seen a sheep die with your own eyes and it isn't on an Afrikaner-owned farm, you may not be able to claw your way back to the borders of Caucasity. Do not gamble with your whiteness in such a reckless way!

Part 2

Live
the
part

Live
the
part
Live
the
part
Live
the
part

7

Kelz's State of the Nation

This part of my guide is not so much a means to help you achieve the desired level of Caucasity. Rather, it is an educational chapter that aims to teach you the truths about our country.

This is a bible that you can use as a reference any time someone tries to tell you white from wrong. This, more than any of the testaments (Old, New and Jewish), is an absolutely crucial guide to your thoughts and feelings as a Caucasian adult.

Unfortunately, if you disagree with any of these very important teachings, you might as well throw the whole guide away because there will be no point. There is no going forward with your Caucasian conversion and trying to adapt to your new world if you do not subscribe to these prescripts.

Let me start off by saying that it gives me great pleasure to be able to correct many of the strange things the history books say. Obviously, the Great White Hope and Leader Eternal has been doing her bit on Twitter since straight after the elections, and even before, to correct history anyway.

A quick note on that, from observing such a significant struggle icon as she. It is important to put on a mask of who you want the public to think you are so that you may gather positive public opinion from even the people you care the least about – black people, in this case. Unfortunately, they are in the majority and there is nothing we can do until we finally ascend to Caucasian heaven – Australia.

She realised that it is almost impossible to do business unless you have the support of those pesky millions and that, even though they cannot help financially because they are all poor and they cannot help intellectually because they are lazy thinkers, they can help if your business is voting numbers.

Leader Eternal has always presented an image of the white saviour Oprah. Now Dina Lohan, mother of Lindsay, also got given that nickname – so you know it's presented to white women who *truly* effect change, even if by mistake or inadvertently.

Leader Eternal herself and my fellow Caucasians have bestowed the title upon her of *the* freedom fighter who single-handedly saved black people from apartheid. Many people use the example of her work as a young journalist who exposed the truth behind the Steve Biko murder to the white public. Then there was some pageant where she had to parade around in a beautiful black sash as a badge of honour; hers was a well-hidden racism.

Now, this is a racism that does not use the k-word or call black people monkeys. Rather, it is a tiny racism. It is one that hates affirmative action and doubts the qualifications of any black person in charge, but at the same time only hires black people as a token. It is a beautiful kind of racism that I seek to perfect because it smiles at you, takes your votes or your business and then calls you incompetent when you resist it.

But let me not go further down this side street.

As part of my amazing history lesson, I will go as far back as when South Africa started and correct many of the urban legends (😒 colonialism 😒) so that everyone will have a more accurate idea of this country. It is no longer okay to be judged by something that not only happened, like, years ago, but also was grossly exaggerated to fit the victim mentality that plagues black people at the moment. Gosh, they just love playing the victim so much – unlike white people, who are the *actual* victims. White people now have to *work* for what they have and that is simply unfair! You say equality, we say oppression!

There are three main headings under which South Africa's estimated thousand-year history can be categorised – True South Africans, Colonialism and Apartheid.

If you are black, your first instinct (like I saw with Supreme Leader) will be to fight and say my categories are wrong. But if you put down your fighting spears and shields, listen to the message between the message (that is not confusing) and really just *think about it*, then you will understand that my wisdom is here to protect you and to help you realise that you have been getting it wrong the whole time.

Listen to your favourite Caucasian personalities, especially the ones you people claim are racist. The whites have all the answers because they did not have Bantu education telling them the wrong things; they read and engage and you people just react and sing and dance.

And as Belinda Bozzoli once (correctly) tweeted: 'Their persistent and relentlessly deafening singing of struggle songs is really irritating . . . Its symbolic and non-literate forms (songs, dance, gestures) seem to matter more than clever words and well-crafted arguments.' (Note that the tweet appeared without the use of hyphens, so in the interest of not dumbing down the essential message, I have added them. I know she meant them to be there.)

All this is to say that, while white people are thinkers and intellectuals who do not need hyphens to prove it, blacks sing, dance and make aggressive gestures reminiscent of cavemen. That is why you cannot trust anything they have written.

Wow, how easy it is for me to get lost in the amazing thought leadership that is the Democratic Alliance. But let me get back to the subject at hand – our history lesson.

True South Africans

According to many Caucasian folks, the only true South Africans are the Khoi or San peoples. This is because most of us are taught that they are no longer around and disappeared at about the same time as the dinosaurs. It is hard to decipher what they are saying in those rock paintings of theirs, so they could be anywhere. Even living among us.

I have also heard that the Coloured community is them rebranded. Kind of like how FW is rebranding from the guy who open-heartedly freed TarTar, to the guy who wishes he had locked him up in the first place. A stronger individual who will not be bullied into hiding his

truth. God bless Africa that man. Even though he is ashamed of what that peace prize stands for, he still has it, so suck on that lemon, ha!

The only reason the topic of true South Africans is ever even brought up is because my chinas (slang alert, I don't actually know any Chinese people) use it to deflect from any irritating and nonsensical conversations about land expropriation with or without compensation. We all know that the Khoi people sold their land for the kokis they used to become famous rock-painting artists. Caucasians have managed to keep the land in their families for generations, the Khoi and San have disappeared or transformed, and now black people think they have any claim to it? The same black people who migrated south from Ghana, or whatever.

How dare they compare our rightful and helpful colonialism (to improve their lives, mind you) to their intrusive 'natural' migration?

There is no real way of seeing who was here first (there was no Instagram) or checking whether the migration was natural or unnatural, and that's unfortunate. All we can do is choose who we want to believe and I don't know about you but I choose to believe the people who wrote my high school history textbook – EF van der Merwe and SG Geldenhuys, thanks you guys!

Colonialism

You have most probably heard the one-sided story that colonialism can *only* be a negative thing. Now, that would be the black side of the coin that does not appreciate the good things that come with the bad.

Colonialism **✗**
is only bad

Benefits:
- English **✔**
- Formal education
- Tarred roads

A small, personal example: I was planning a birthday party for my best friend, Michaela. But her parents announced that they were getting divorced the day before but I had already paid for the venue and the suppliers, and everyone had RSVP'd and booked the date.

Anyway, when Michaela got to the party we yelled 'Surprise!' and it was the most fabulous night anyone had ever experienced. She spent most of the night being ungrateful and in tears about her parents and then called me selfish and awful for having gone ahead with the party. In my opinion, *she* was the awful one because she failed to focus on the good of the party. The stress from her parents fighting had made her lose weight, so she looked incredible, and every single person said it was such a fun night.

Now, this is *exactly* what it feels like when people are ungrateful about colonialism. Yes, the timing and murders and slavery was off, but the gifts that came with it trump the negatives and *that* is what people should be focusing on. I mean, of course we understand that genocide and forced enslavement, families being ripped apart and losing all your worldly possessions in your own country must be super irritating, but guys, at least now you drive on tar roads and don't live in the jungle and stuff.

As the Leader Eternal once tweeted: 'Do you genuinely believe the legacy of colonialism was ONLY negative? Then let's scrap the constitution including concepts such as the separation of powers. Let's scrap formal education institutions, the English language, etc., etc. . . .'

Anyone who wants to counter these points with 'facts' must be dreaming. Schooling was invented by the ancient Romans and even though they did not colonise England and the Netherlands to pass it on, we would not have listened had the latter two nations not come and violently forced themselves on us.

It was for our own good, like when your parents give you a hiding to make you a better person. And of course, we would not have English. Even though you think speaking black languages would have been fine, how would we understand white people when they told us what to do?

Anyway, you get the point. It was all for our own good.

Of course, my reverse-racist mom is like, 'Well, Ethiopia was not colonised and they have all the infrastructure any country has because globalisation would have happened without the murdering,' and I'm like, 'Hellooowa! Ethiopia has so many flies! Soooo #thinkaboutit'.

And because my dad defends anything my mom says, he goes on, 'Also, Africa and black people actually invented a lot, if not most, of the advancements and infrastructure you speak about.'

Sigh, and again I have to remind them that, unless Van der Merwe and Geldenhuys wrote about it, it cannot be true. He also made me watch *Hidden Figures* to try to prove the point that black people were integral to many industrial advancements but that movie was boring and at the end of the day, no. Just no.

Apartheid

The dreaded a-word makes for the third major category of South African history. Apartheid is by far the most misunderstood concept in the South African lexicon and this makes me very sad. If, for once, you actually applied your mind and not your emotions, you would understand some things are not as dramatic as your families would like you to believe.

What is important to note is that things left in the past should remain there. Why do you people always look back instead of looking forward? Are you owls? Didn't think so. The only way we can pretend apartheid never happened and therefore remove all white guilt (which is not free and fair, like our elections, but let me not go there) is to move *forward*.

You'll also note that always having to remember the past is only applicable to the times when Coloured and black people were victims. Why do they always insist on special treatment? Of course, it does not apply to actual tragedies like the two world wars, which we should commemorate and never ever forget.

How many times must my group say sorry for things, especially those that took place when they weren't even born yet? Like, if my grandfather kidnapped, murdered, stole from and forcibly removed you, and if my generational wealth is a result of that, why must *I* say sorry? Why should I be punished and give everything back? That is not how it works.

Not that I am saying this is what apartheid was, because it's not.

Here is something to think about. If black people did not *want* apartheid and they were in the majority, why did they not just, like, say no or fight or something? You know why? Because they could see the benefits, but of course they know if they complain, they'll get rewarded.

It's like this one time I hit, or let me rather say 'bumped into', an annoying girl with my car. She was totally fine – that is, until she was told she could potentially get money out of me. All of a sudden, she was talking about scars being left behind and how she is at a disadvantage because she has trauma and a limp. Anyway, her complaints and dramatics won her the case and I have had to pay reparations ever since. That is exactly like this apartheid thing.

How to pretend apartheid never happened

Move forward. Forget about the past

Apartheid was essentially just a list of rules to abide by. Now all of a sudden everyone can simply do whatever they want. Does this mean I should let a child drink simply because I can? Not everyone can have the same rules because not everyone is the same.

> Black people were built for servitude

Black people were built for servitude . . . that is why they have broader shoulders and bigger knuckles. This has been anthropologically confirmed, so don't come to me saying I'm speaking untruths just because your feelings might be a little hurt by it. Structurally, they also have backs that curve more for a better cleaning position. Only thing is, they have larger nostrils so they can't walk for too long in leafy suburbs because the pollen affects them. That is why there was a curfew under apartheid when they needed to get out the suburbs – it's because pollen is most active at night.

This is why I say these rules were put in place for their protection. It's like when our parents say we can't go out at night. It wasn't to irritate or imprison them, it was actually for *their* benefit.

These days FW de Klerk is getting a bad reputation for being outspoken about how he really feels about black people and the things they do. Why? Because black people would rather he pretend apartheid was not for their own good. Guys, remember, Nelson Mandela held his hand. Would he have done that if De Klerk was racist or a bad guy? You should really think before you speak.

And a lot of people are always talking about reparations and how they are owed things. How about you work hard: then maybe you won't feel like things should just be handed to you? I will go into more detail in the progress (LOL) report that follows below, but I simply do not understand what black people want from whites when whites have already given them freedom and an apology.

You people. Honestly, give you a hand and you grab a whole arm(ed struggle).

Now that I have cleared that up, I will give a progress report, kinda like Coconut Kelz's State of the Nation address. You will also find the report on my blog: coconutkelz.cocothoughts. wordpress/myopinion/wellhelensopinionreally_gov/think-aboutit.

This year happens to be a big anniversary as it is 25 years since the end of apartheid (boo! I know!). So, this year's report is my most scathing one to date. Hold on to your ZCC badges because I am going in.

White privilege

White privilege is the boogeyman for the woke black . . . the Pinky Pinky (it is for them to catch the reference), if you will. They firmly believe in its existence and are scared of it, and it also gives them sleepless nights. But guess what, people . . . those of us who are actually smart know *it is not real!*

All my friends are white and let me tell you, even though they are all rich and have amazing jobs and went to good schools, it does not mean they are privileged. I mean, there were loads of black people at our school. Four, to be exact. So, where is the privilege if they were also there?

Anyway, most of my friends' dads grew up poor by white standards (which means they weren't millionaires and only had two family cars, which weren't even nice cars). They did not necessarily have any qualifications but they worked their way up to the top. What further proof do you need that hard work gets you everywhere?

If you're anything like my reverse-racist family, I already know what you're thinking: 'Well, that is what happens when only white people could compete for jobs.'

But hellooo, not only did they work hard, but they also really wanted it. Also, don't come to me with your stories about nepotism. It's only called nepotism or a handout when black people are involved. Jemma's dad appointing her boyfriend as CEO of the firm does not make it nepotism. Unlike, say, Zuma's son, Jemma's boyfriend would have got the position even if her dad wasn't CEO because he worked his way up for months and months from being an intern.

The other day I read this horrible comment on the page of one of my favourite YouTubers. In trying to take Helen on in the debate about white privilege, he was spewing the greatest load of one-sided nonsense. I will post the whole comment and then discuss for 10 marks, as the black youth say:

> White privilege for a small example is being in a store and not being followed by security because there's an assumption you'll steal. It's walking past a car and not having the people inside lock their doors as you pass.

White privilege:

- Not being followed by security
- Not being lied to
- Not being corrupt
- Not being called rioters or protesters
- Not being forced to learn a black language
- Not getting less money when applying for loans
- Not being called lazy
- Not having your name changed

It's being able to book a table at any restaurant and not being lied to that it's fully booked when they hear your accent, but when you call back seconds later with an affected accent, there's plenty of space. It's people calling for removal of illegal immigrants but only meaning the African ones.

It's people putting the spotlight on the ANC's corruption but completely ignoring Steinhoff, Absa and plenty of the white monopoly capital corruption that is quietly exposed but ignored daily. And it is called 'accounting irregularities' when white people do it.

It's black people being called rioters or protesters and white people doing the same thing being called marchers. The difference in terms comes with a difference of media and police reaction. It's black and white men committing the same crime but black men getting harsher sentences.

It's black people being forced to learn English and sometimes Afrikaans but white people won't even learn half of one of our languages and yet they will ask us why we speak English if we don't like colonialism as if they can't do any critical thinking about the way English and Afrikaans were violently beaten and imposed on us . . . And they don't need to learn any vernacular languages because our education and work is conducted in white colonial languages.

It's a white couple applying for a loan and getting more money than a black couple because our skin makes us a risk.

It's black people beginning their commute to work in people's homes and shops at 4 a.m., leaving their kids to get ready and to school by themselves and still being called lazy and being told they must work harder.

It's white people reporting a 'suspicious black male' because they dared to walk on 'their' street, even though the pass laws of apartheid are supposed to have been removed.

It's being called 'Lee' when your name is Lesego because white teachers or bosses can't be bothered to learn to pronounce it. That is just the tip of the iceberg. Stop reducing it to basic shit like money. Privilege is more than that.

My response? Ummm, no, it's not like that. It *is* only about the money. Don't make it about anything more. And Lee is a much better name than Lesego, anyway, so I would think about changing it permanently. Jeez, you get shot for good ideas around here.

Thinking the phantom of white privilege is real is the thing that is actually holding you people back. And yet you think if you harp on and on about it, we will suddenly also start believing it is real? Even if you offer more examples of other forms of privilege, forms other than money, they can easily be countered. If I claim the sky is green and I get a whole lot of people to agree with me and then I say I want to be compensated for the blue-sky lie, does it not mean I should be?

I didn't get up this morning thinking I would be dropping these truth bombs but someone has to do it. #thinkaboutit

Black privilege

Now I have to move on to the part of my progress report that isn't easy to write about, because people are always contradicting me on this. But it is real and it is called black privilege.

There were many moments when I was writing this guide when I thought, I could just as well have asked Helen to write it because some of the chapters are completely inspired by her teachings. Her likeness should be made into statues and I cannot wait for the day you all realise she was racist right all along.

Black man: 'You clearly don't understand white privilege. We had plenty technology here that was eroded/annihilated by colonialism. You did us zero favours by colonising us.'

HOW DARE HE?! Clearly someone needs this guide. Please buy it for him.

Well, he got the wrong person riled up because Hell (that's what we call the Eternal Leader for short) got wind of it and removed her election mask to answer him.

Helen: 'Well you clearly don't understand black privilege. It is being able to loot a country and steal hundreds of billions and get re-elected. If ppl [she knows cool slang] want permanent poverty for the masses they are going about it the right way #BlackPrivilege.'

First of all, Queen Hell has no idea how liberated we all felt after she tweeted that. Finally, we could be racist without being persecuted for it. My friends are really happy because now they get to say what they want and be as racist honest as possible without the Twitter police coming after them.

Remember, they don't see colour with me, but colour sees them.

Just to translate because all of you lost your shit: 'Only black people have ever been corrupt. No governments other than black ones have ever looted and stolen and been re-elected. Not even the apartheid government. They may have had accounting irregularities, but those were honest mistakes. They may have kidnapped, killed and systemically damaged the nation but hello #Stompie.'

In short, corruption is what black people do. Corruption derives from the Greek word '*eruptos*', which means black. So it is virtually impossible for corruption ever to be about white people. Also, white people are super honest and just don't lie, so there's that.

• • • • • • • • • • • •

Corruption

Greek – *eruptos*,
black

• • • • • • • • • • • •

As an aside: accounting irregularities are when you make a mistake and accidentally pay money into your account instead of into a business account (these things can happen). Or when you maybe take a donation and then it turns out it was a bribe – you couldn't have known! They also happen when you blow millions under the guise of being honest because, luckily, white skin gets that assumption. How were you supposed to know CEOs can't use the company accounts? I mean, since when?

To conclude today's history lesson and State of the Nation report: colonialism and apartheid may be what made you poor but hey, 25 years is more than enough time to fix 400 years of damage! If you stopped complaining and opened your eyes, you'd realise that the real thieves weren't colonialists or the apartheid regime – they are the current black looters in power. White privilege is a figment of black people's imagination, but black privilege is real. Whoever said history was boring or difficult to understand? It's this easy.

• • • • • • • • • • • •
White
privilege =
A figment of
black people's
imagination
• • • • • • • • • • • •

8

BEE(tch), please!
How to be a madam

In life, there will be several moments when you'll realise you were born to be a boss. If you are white, this will happen at birth; depending on whether you are English or Afrikaans, you will be boss or the more prestigious *baas*. If you are not white, however, this will be something that you will have to practise as part of the programme to lead you up to and through the pearly gates on Mount Caucasity.

As with most goals mentioned in this guide, becoming a boss is achievable but not always easy. As some black rapper probably said, 'It pays the cost to be da boss!', which I suppose can be translated as, you have to sacrifice in order to achieve significance. For instance, there will be moments when you will have to be quite harsh to people around you but who said it was easy to achieve boss status?

As with most things in life, there are different categories of bosshood, so I will discuss how to be a boss both at home and at work. Let's first look at a few basic guidelines for how to be the boss at home.

The first thing you are going to need here is staff. Now, the wonderful thing is that staff are no longer limited to visibly white people. Even the darker-hued citizens of our country have invested in someone to clean for them.

The thing that makes this type of labour so necessary is that we live such busy lives. Even those of you who are lucky to be home executives (previously known as housewives) will be doing yoga, shopping or supervising the gardener. Having staff is your right. After all, this is what we fought for as a nation. The right to exploit human beings for our own comfort.

Now, when you are on the hunt for your very own *sisi*, you must try to find one with a backstory that is desperate enough for you not have to pay her a fair wage, but not so desperate that she steals from you. Obviously, nanny cam will take care of any suspicions you might have; so you become either an amazing detective who saved her own belongings, or a weird voyeur with a feather-duster fetish.

Where was I? Ah yes, finding your very own *sisi*. The best places to look are in your friends' little black books (the books are not necessarily black, although they can be, but the 'black' here refers to the service providers).

The second-best place to look is at bus depots. My favourite is Park Station. Now, I am way too aware of the crime in our cities to go myself, but I will send a driver or my ghetto cousin to go scout for me. She also knows more languages than I do so she can approach them and explain what we are looking for and are offering.

This is a good thing to keep in mind, by the way. Even

though you want to escape the black hole that was your up-bringing, there are a few key people from your past who will prove to be assets, so you should keep them around. Mostly, they speak English well, went to a former model C school and have some kind of job so that you know they are not there to *tshontsha* (steal from) you. They must also be family, so that there is a bit of an obligation to hang out with each other.

Another place to look for a new maid, helper or domestic worker, as these overly politically correct agents want you to call them – I mean, it doesn't change the fact that we are going to continue to underpay them so much so that their work could be confused for slave labour, but yes, let us focus on what we *call* them. Honestly, you guys! Anyway, you can also look for your *sisi* in the homes or phonebooks of your friends – poaching is perfectly fine. It's not like they'll recognise them when they come over anyway. We don't look staff in the eye: so that they always remember their place, and to prevent familiarity. Cleaning is usually genetic, so when you have found one, keep close to her family so that should she die or just get lazy, you can *lahla* her (throw her away) and get her sister or daughter to come fill her incompetent shoes.

Okay, so now you have hired her. 'Where will she live?' you may ask yourself. There are two answers, depending on your tax bracket. The first option is that she will live in a very small room at the back of your huge property. We call this the servant's quarters (because 'slave quarters' has more of an American ring to it: #LocaliseIt). She may have a child or two whom you allow to live there. This gives you the opportunity to take them to school, which will make you feel better about the fact that you pay their mom close to nothing. She dare complain, though, because you have let her stay (in a room probably bigger than her shack) and nothing will stop you from enjoying your moment of feeling pretty damn generous. Hello! Free board!

Having someone live in a small room at the back of your property also comes in handy in the event of a break-in. Of course, since you will lock the burglar bars and gates of the main house, you will literally have nothing to fear. Either her screams will alert you and you will still have time to get away, or the thieves will get so distracted by taking her stuff, they won't even get to you . . . So, it goes without saying that

Helpful Cupid tip:
Maids love gardeners and security guards

you should stock up her room with unnecessary but crime-attracting items.

The second option is for her to commute. This depends on where she is from and/or how resourceful she is. My last *sisi* was from Zimbabwe, so commuting wasn't an option. That is, until we totes introduced her to one of our security guards and they hit it off (helpful Cupid tip: maids love gardeners and security guards, and vice versa). Now she is living somewhere that still makes her late for work, but at least keeps her off the property until I can build that trust, which will probably be never.

The only thing about the commuting girls is that they rarely arrive on time and have oh so many excuses for why they are late with my sunrise cuppa. Without it, I am a stress ball and she knows it, so why she won't wake up earlier, I just don't know. Almost like she doesn't appreciate this amazing opportunity. Anyway, her disciplinary hearing is next week and good luck to her!

A good time to receive your Morning Joe is 6 a.m. because you're defs not a morning person without it, grrr! LOLz. Given that it takes about thirty minutes to make the coffee (I think), she should be brewing from 5:30 a.m. And that's generous given that I actually get up and update my blog at 5:45 a.m. in the summer but you know, 'legal rights' or whatever. Not to say slavery is right, but boy did it have some benefits. I guess now you can see where Helen was coming from with the colonisation theory.

Once awake, you need to drop the kids off at school before going to yoga, or just go to yoga, if you still live a carefree, childless life. This gives *sisi* enough time to clean up your room and disappear from the first floor so that you don't have to watch her clean and feel guilty. Yoga is very important, you guys . . . where else are you going to wear your famous leggings? I mean, obviously you need to wear them on days when you don't feel like going to yoga either, so that the people in Woolies think you went and they welcome you with open quinoa.

Now you need to hire an unattractive gardener – I know that sounds like an unnecessary qualification but trust me, to a maid, there are also hot gardeners. The reason he needs to be unattractive to black people is so that neither he nor *sisi* are distracted on the job. In fact, if possible, hire siblings or a couple that's been married for a long time. (Side note: remember to give them the house rules, because no matter what the relationship, the gardener is never allowed to come inside. He has to use the toilet in *sisi*'s room because . . . germs. Even *sisi* may only use her own toilet.)

Gardeners and maids love eating off enamel crockery (not that they have much time to eat but give them a big lunch so they don't die on the job, 😐), so you're going to want to buy a set. Pick n Pay had lovely 'maid' and 'gardener' cups earlier

Enamel crockery

Gardeners and maids love eating off these

this year which, even though the blacks lost their shit, I thought were actually pretty useful because who doesn't love a mug that is made specially for them?

Last year I got a 'world's worst daughter' mug (as a joke of course) and I'm grateful because no one touches my mug . . . because it is labelled. You know when someone at the office uses your mug? Well, the back room is the office of the maid and gardener, so imagine that.

When you dismiss them for the day, you need to be strict but fair. To get as close as possible to the promised land of milk and Caucasity, you should remind your staff that your trust must be earned. So, when they leave, check the bags they came with. Theft should be nipped in the bud. I once caught my maid stealing leftovers. She said it was for her children but I know a *sgebenga* when I see one, so I said *hayi-*

khona! The thing is, you give these people an arm and next thing they are stealing laptops, clothing, teaspoons or even something as simple as bricks to put under their beds for protection from whatever mythical creature is trending that month.

Now, things work a little differently when it comes to being a boss at work. This is because of pesky departments like Human Resources, which is always trying to enforce boring rules like that horrible BEE. So now you have to hire Them or face heavy fines.

They are not to be trusted and, as in your home, you will need a nanny cam. This is not only to expose any thieving, but also, most importantly, to catch the gossip. Show the recordings to your *sisi* and tell her to translate all the office gossip. There's nothing you can technically do about it or you'll have to admit to the presence of the cams but at least you'll know who to trust. Generally, just shout at your team often enough that they may only speak in English because this isn't a shebeen and then they should get the point.

While we're talking about the office environment, there are a few things you will have to move away from as you ascend into the great, white beyond.

Firstly, the kind of food you bring to work will definitely define you. But before we even get there, you should know that what you call the container you keep your food in is already part of the social group areas act. Only if you are very black will you call it a *skhaftin*. That is the defiant kind of black who probably talks very loud and, despite multiple reprimands, is always late.

The kind of food you'll be most likely to find in a *skhaftin* is of the more traditional variety. Now, it needs to be said that both super-Caucasian and super-black foods will smell but the smell of wet towel is better than the smell of sheep innards. Really, *that* is what they bring to the office! It's like they *want* us to be racist. Anyway, things like walkie-talkies, tripe, pap, etc., those are the foods that you can expect to be exposed to when someone calls their lunch container a *skhaftin*.

You also get those who call it Tupperware (regardless of whether the container is the actual Tupperware brand or not). The first thing to note is that, although this group is not as bad as the first group, there is still a not-so-kosher aura about them. These ones may be able to cross over into Caucasity like you (if they wanted it badly enough) but they choose to be

Skhaftin
Very black definition – container for traditional foods like walkie-talkies, tripe and pap

woke so, like, whatevs. They usually don't carry stinky food unless they had a wedding or funeral over the weekend. This group tends to enjoy leftovers from their culinary flops. Think curries and stews, oxtail in winter. You will know which one is theirs even after office *sisi* washes them, because they will have a permanent orange stain from all that oil they use. Fun fact: blacks love their oil.

The third group (and this is the one you should aspire to,

if you are not there already) calls the container a lunchbox. Note, however, that it shouldn't be *one* box. It should be multiple containers neatly packed into a small cooler bag. You should literally have a minimum of eight containers in the bag, each smaller and more arbitrary than the other.

For instance, say you'll be making a tuna salad for lunch. One container will be for salt, the other for pepper, and yet another for the salad dressing. You will also need a smaller container for your daily vitamins and aesthetics medication. Finally, there's a container for your crushed Provita – remember, only one a day.

The good Caucasian worker aspiring to be a boss will also always have a water bottle on her desk, filled with a little gin and topped with white tears. White tears are the amazing collection of molecules that are emitted whenever the chosen ones complain about something that is totally not real, like white privilege or a lack of managers.

Now, being a boss at work and navigating through your Caucasian conversion will not be easy. Black people will try everything to distract you from your goal, including throwing a boy (or girl) who cries wolf at you. You know the folk tale, right? As a refresher, long, long ago there was a shepherd who worked for a farmer and his family. One day, he got so bored he decided to fake a wolf attack on the farmer's flock. He screamed for the family to come. It must've been in, like, the 1990s coz nowadays they can surely just Uber or even better, Instagram live the attack to alert people. But the thing is, it was a fake attack, of course.

When the farmer got there he was totes furious because he'd had to get there on foot and it was hot and farms are huge. My friend Stace's family has a farm. You guys . . . H-U-G-E. After the shepherd had tried his silly trick, like, two more times, one day a real wolf came (FYI, this farm is in like America or Nazareth or wherever wolves are).

Once again, he screamed for people to come, but this time neither the farmer nor the townspeople (honestly, that's what they call them) believed him and all the sheep got killed. The end.

What was the point of all this? Oh right! People who always cry racism. Same concept. Race cards are the most over-played in any deck. Especially the office deck. Take two for time-wasting.

People who call out racism only do so when they are, in fact, in the wrong but don't want to admit it. Racism is not real (unless it is reverse racism), so when some black in the office logs a complaint, take it with a pinch of salt. Their sense of entitlement will mean that, even when the boss is rightfully calling them lazy monkeys, they will cry racism. Just write down what they are saying and promise to escalate and investigate it. You have no idea what that means because there is no investigative unit but it will make them think something is going to happen and you won't get reported to an ombudsman or something and get into trouble.

People tend to believe the person with the better accent and closer proximity to whiteness, so don't worry too much about the he said, she said. Just mention your school or at least someone you know who went to a top private school and watch how the case disappears. The CCMA can be a scary thing, but it could also stand for Caucasian Conversations Matter Altogether when you make it work to your advantage.

Another pointer to get you closer to bosshood is to hire the right kind of security guards. Make sure that you get the most entitled ones to work for you. Ideally, they should display disdain for black people, especially black youths. This will not be registered as racism because it will be coming from a fellow melanated muppet.

They should have no patience for any nonsense or horseplay and must have a bad attitude in general. A super-intense relationship with clipboards is another important characteristic.

The very best of them wear a badge with a silver star on green and black felt material. This means they do very good work in the security industry and do not tolerate 'muckaboutery'. However, you will have to find temporary replacements for them over the Easter period because they all disappear to a place called Moria, which I think is the training ground for security companies.

● ● ● ● ● ● ● ● ● ● ● ● ●

Ngamla

boss or baas – the pinnacle of being a Caucasian

● ● ● ● ● ● ● ● ● ● ● ● ●

I trust that the information in this chapter will help you be the very best boss or *baas* the world never knew it needed. When you get elevated to *ngamla* position (as my *sisi* says) then you are basically Caucasian and you have reached the summit of all that life can possibly offer.

9

Be your best do-gooder

There are many different ways to do 'good' deeds but, as with everything else, not all good deeds are equal. Furthermore, for many of us the end goal is the reward . . . but the kind of reward and when it will be received is usually the main differentiating factor. This is what separates the 'donors' from the 'charity workers', for example. One carries prestige and honour and the other, well, it denotes that the person involved is still poor.

This chapter offers a guide to how to be a do-gooder in a way that will get your name onto library entrances in the future and into the hearts of white people everywhere.

Let me give you an example. A few months ago, one Monet van Deventer (I could not make that name up even if I tried: sounds like a fine arts student who does striptease to pay for her studies) went to fill up her car but didn't have any Monet-money on her. A very kind and surprisingly gentle black man called Nkosikho (I think his name means Petroleum Giver in isiVernac) offered to pay for her petrol so that she could get home safely.

Now, I think it is important to add here that it was most definitely her very white skin that made her seem trustworthy and honest. She clearly was a damsel in distress. I mean, if this story was about, say, a Lesego Tlhabi, the assumption would have been that she was a chancer who didn't have the money but insisted on filling up anyway.

Remember, some people are simply more blessed than others. And these blessings usually come raining down on white people or people who help white people. Monet Teresa (as I affectionately call her) then set up a crowdfunding page for Nkosikho which aimed to raise R100 000 but ultimately raised over R400 000. This is quite amazing because I usually only tip about R1. Give them any more and they might buy drugs or something!

Anyway, the crowdfunding page obviously caught on to the inherent deviousness that befalls all black men at birth. It decided that it would not give Nkosikho the cash directly, which, as we expected, made Black Twitter very angry. Extremely aggressive, as usual.

What they forgot, though, is that we are taught to give the homeless food instead of money because you cannot trust what they will do with the latter. All they want is bling bling or substances to abuse. This is not my opinion, it is fact.

You just can't trust them to make good decisions – or any decisions, actually, but especially decisions involving money. This is why God made them poor. He knew that they would misuse money, so He gave it to white people and a select group of black folk who have Caucasian aspirations or interests.

● ● ● ● ● ● ● ● ● ● ● ● ●

Fact

Food money
used for
bling bling
or substance
abuse

● ● ● ● ● ● ● ● ● ● ● ● ●

The reason I am telling you this story is because I want you to see the difference between a white saviour and a black one. Two people did good in this story, but it was Monet who was seen as the charitable one. Nkosikho was not even expected to do something so selfless and he was merely thrust into the spotlight to help tell the story of white generosity.

It is a widely known fact that black people actually enjoy not being given opportunities. After all, even the tithe in the poorest churches still goes to white Jesus . . . that is simply the circle of life. If you think about it, aren't all Caucasians white Jesus? Exactly.

In short, there are many different ways in which one can commit to being a do-gooder, but some deeds are 'gooder' than others. In this chapter, I will outline the deeds that are most important and most revered by my fellow whites, and which will therefore be better rewarded.

Another difference to keep in mind in this business of doing good is that white people get rewarded in this lifetime but black people only get theirs in the afterlife. Plot twist: they still won't, LOLz.

Charity work

There are so many things you can do to be considered a charitable person. So many ways to receive even more than you could give.

Firstly, the kind of charity you choose is crucial. The only way to move closer to whiteness is to focus on animals – wildlife especially but domestic animals too. Even volunteering at the SPCA, for example, will

earn you much adulation from your peers and peer hopefuls.

The best charity to get involved in by far is anything to do with rhinos. Unfortunately, it is no longer a trend but back in the day putting a red plastic horn on the front of your car was a very clear indication of the levels your Caucasity was at.

Some people might ask, why, with so many poor and orphaned children in South Africa, should they choose animal-related charities? The answer is quite simple: charities that look after South African children will most likely be filled with the future *sgebengas* of this country, so why aid them in getting there faster? Why feed the monkeys, as they say? Unless you are talking about real monkeys, then yes, of course, feed them and adopt them and they will make for a great and loyal and super-cute pet.

Animals are more important to white people, which is why they are such an elevated race. Remember the scale of importance? It always starts with white people, followed by dogs and rhinos as well as a few other things and ends with black people. To be your best do-gooder, it's vital that you help animals first. Don't upset the species hierarchy – you really *do not* want anyone to assume you might be a black.

If you ever need to justify yourself (only black people might question you in this regard), you can always use the same reasoning we are all taught at indoctrination induction: 'Animals are helpless to defend themselves.' Yes, I know, you could say the same thing about children, but black children are different. Just think about how, when a teenage boy gets shot by police – usually after he has done something wrong like look at them with scheming thoughts – he is referred to as a man. It's the same as R. Kelly's alleged victims who were referred to as young women. But then you have Ryan Lochte or Brett Kavanaugh being referred to as boys who 'will be boys'.

These wonderful privileges and more can be yours at the low cost of R99,99 if you call the hotline now on 0861-MAKE-ME-YT. You also receive a get-off-on-all-charges-free card (charges like 'driving while black' or 'making black noise in white spaces'). So do not delay, call today!

A really beautiful thing about attaining Caucasity and surviving this shithole is that your intentions and actions are never questioned. In fact, even if you are recorded calling someone the k-word or all evidence unequivocally points to your guilt in a crime, you will still be presumed innocent. Someone must have framed you.

So, this guide is not just about the aesthetics of pale living. It's also about highlighting the benefits and privileges that are paramount to living your best shit-free life.

Praise and worship

There are many different ways in which people choose to honour their beliefs and become a good person. But believe it or not, even *this* is divided among racial lines.

You need to know that, when you articulate your beliefs to someone, they will immediately place you in a box that is very difficult to escape from. It is like a Pandora's box, but for race. People will assume things about your tax bracket, your social status, and even your ability to do certain jobs based on your religious beliefs.

Usually, saying you are Christian is enough, but there are various denominations under this wide umbrella. Each will have a different impact on what kind of person you are perceived to be. Also, there are definitely some branches of Christianity that you do not want to find yourself exploring. For example, ZCC is the religion of the gardener. If you want to be taken seriously at all and have any chance of graduating to whiter heights, you will have to give this one a skip. I mean, they always take busses and taxis to Limpopo over Easter . . . is that the kind of future you see for yourself? The Kruger is soooo wonderful at that time of the year, but that's not where they are going. Yiiikes!

> ZCC =
> Religion of
> the gardener

Your Caucasian conversion might require you to make tough decisions because it could potentially mean letting go of your entire belief system and adopting one that is more in line with the kind of person you seek to become. After all, you want people to make the right kind of assumptions about you.

Great examples of Christianity are: the NG Kerk.

NG Kerk = A purist church

Now, this church might sound intimidating because it is synonymous with apartheid, but that is actually a good thing. Even though Coloured people now want to claim Afrikaans as their language (😳), the NG Kerk is still a purist church at heart. The only problem is that you obviously have to be fluent in that language. Also, I was not too well received the one time my friend, Susan, tried to take me. I don't think I had been to enough bleaching sessions, though, so I don't quite blame them . . . I still looked, by and large, like a black. I will have to go to the NG Kerk again soon to determine whether my treatments have been successful.

You see, they don't hold back on the truth, which is easily the best thing about the place. You're either in or you're out . . . no fakeness here like with my group of 'friends' (yes, I'm talking about you, Ash-'liar' – that's what we call Ashley behind her back).

Now, the NG Kerk is a good place for just getting away from your everyday shithole troubles and is an amazing place for opportunities if you want to get into farming or if you work at an Afrikaans company. Even if you are just dating an Afrikaans man – go, so that the parents can see you and feel '*Sy's oukei, nie soos die ander swart mense nie* (she's okay, not like the other blacks)'.

Anglican
church =
A decent
example of
Christianity

Methodist
and Roman
Catholic
church =
Filled with
black brethren

Another decent example of Christianity is the Anglican church. Be careful of both the Methodist and the Roman Catholic church – they're filled with our black brethren. Those missionaries really did their utmost to make sure they did a good job to get into white heaven but my goodness, it's like the holy bread is actually filling or something. They come as if it's a whole free meal!

Anyway, the Anglican church is way more subdued and staid and as it falls under the Church of England (the Queen's church), you know it has a stiff upper lip. I needn't explain that the stiff upper lip is associated with the more subtle and micro-racism that has filled our offices and schools today.

It is the 'tell people they can't speak their languages here' of religions. The 'if you can say white privilege, then I can say black privilege' of denominations. Even the 'get over apartheid, it is in the past!' of spiritual homes. Everything about this paradise screams white privilege and it is joyous. But not in the loud way. Even the songs are sung at a level of a passionate whisper, for here, it is the organ that has power over all.

Most of South Africa's elite schools are Anglican and have very few black people in them, so this should show the commitment this denomination has to maintaining the status quo.

Tradition is most important; unlike at those gaudy charismatic churches that are taking over the country, you will not find BEE blacks here. Even your gay friends will have to sit this one out or pretend to be otherwise. They know why, and they will be okay with it because it is for the greater good.

At Anglican schools, you will mix with white people of a more English background. They will fill the Hiltons and St Anne's of the world and will perfect that passive-aggressive close-mouthed grin known affectionately as 'that white smile'. Nostalgia has me all teary eyed – ah, what great memories!

Every now and then I go back to Our Lady of the Swart Gevaar just to keep that Anglican door open. You never know when you will need a corporate or government job where people tell you at least once a day how well you speak, but don't say the same thing to your white boss who only has a matric.

In this section, we also have to consider atheism, since today many people are atheists, what with science and books getting their time to shine. However, truth be told, it is not important whether or not you believe in something. It's only important that you align yourself with the right people in the right places.

> Atheists
> From the poorer section of the white population

The thing is, atheists are often from the poorer section of the white population. You will not find atheists in higher-up positions in corporate or in governments around the world. It is the religion of people in the arts and people in science. Both interesting groups, but hardly the world's money-makers.

Atheists do not wield any power. I know this because, for a summer, I dove into the world of non-conformism and non-belief and found that, other than having to declare it a few times a day or risk losing any credibility in the atheist world, there was no other place to convene and feel like I was part of something.

Like veganism, atheists need to shout that they are atheist five times a day to a group of people, otherwise they revert to whatever religion they came from. Unlike veganism, it does no one any service to declare that you are an atheist, though . . . again, this is not the religion of the kind of white you should aspire to become.

Judaism
The ultimate religion

Now, the ultimate religion if you want to become aligned with the right kind of Caucasian is Judaism. I feel that goes without saying. I converted to Judaism three years ago. However, although I have had a great time being welcomed into the Caucus Transracial Hebrew Congregation, I couldn't get into a traditional synagogue as I am simply not willing to do the classes and stuff and also, Friday nights are my favourite night to go out.

At the Transracial Congregation, we follow the religious dogma *very* loosely so we veto some of the laws or rules as we go along but are still allowed to partake in the fun parts (it is a special religion with lots of holidays and celebrations). Most importantly, you will be taken more seriously in certain boardrooms when you say you are Jewish. I applied for an internship at Outvestec and within months was promoted because I know some of the more popular prayers.

I have yet to have my Bat Mitzvah but that is only because no one will translate the script into English and it is super tough for me. But fingers crossed, one of the Daniels or Racccch will finally agree to help me and I will be a certified member by year-end – then just watch me become CEO in under five years.

Additionally, Judaism is at least 99.9 per cent white in South Africa so you know you're going to be safe. Their symbol is also a star and I just love stars. I even have them tattooed on me (not the Star of David per se but I'm halfway there due to my affinity for bright, sparkly things).

The only real problem is that amazing bread they make. You guys, I have struggled with my half-vegan, quarter-gluten and paleo diet because challah makes you holla! (You can't see my arms right now but they are doing the 'raising the roof' motion.)

Lastly, I have yet to meet anyone in my synagogue who is poor. They just don't align with that state of being and if you join them you will always be taken care of by the community. I have not been able to date any of the men for longer than three months because every time I speak about meeting their parents, the relationship seems to fade.

Throughout this chapter, you will notice how I did not once mention Islam. That's because it's simply not for you. Because . . . think about it.

● ● ● ● ● ● ● ● ● ● ●
Islam
NOT for you
● ● ● ● ● ● ● ● ● ● ●

10

Put on your political party pants

I am always asked for my opinion on really big news stuff. I am the beacon that all my friends use to shine the light on the truth of politics, race, beauty tips and . . . whatevs.

I'm also a junior Democratic Alliance member in the token department (I'm hoping this guide will get me promoted to senior token). Of course, Mmusi is the most senior token. There's tons of opportunity in the DA so I will continue to spread the good message and impress Helen – she makes all the decisions after all (but I'm sure you knew that). Anyway, I'm getting ahead of myself.

This is my guide to the top three parties and their leaders because you need to know how to conduct yourself when people start talking politics. To complete your Caucasian conversion, you must be clear about who the good guys and the bad guys are.

With the increase in support for the Freedom Front Plus (FF+) , it is clear that there is a yearning for a golden time more than twenty-five years ago where marriages were kept pure and *sgebenga* movement was restricted in our pristine suburbs. They may not be one of the top three parties, but FF+ support is completely acceptable.

Of course, I am a DA member eternal (even if Mmusi seems to be turning on Helen) – there was a ritual and stuff. I can't leave unless I go to 'Harvard' and I'm not going there!

In the following analysis I will be completely free from bias, unlike Euse-BIAS; 702 has become *soooo* captured, you guys! Good thing I'm here to spread the truth.

The EFF

Despite the increased support they got in the national elections, the least important of the big three parties is the Economic Freedom Fighters (EFF). I call them the Economic Fake Front (just a tip here – to make it in politics, you have to be really good at puns: white people love puns).

This party you will recognise by their horrible red overalls. They all dress like gardeners and maids. This already tells you all you need to know about what they want to turn this country into. They want us all to be poor!

> Tip:
> To make it in politics, you have to be really good at puns

Also, the colour red is so very aggressive. I mean, in what colour is the devil usually drawn? Yes, you got it – red.

Furthermore, the leaders *tshontsha* money all the time. How else can Julius drive a Range Rover if he's a gardener? Think about it.

Julius Malema: Julius is president of the EFF and the very definition of a thug. And remember, guys, this is an unbiased and researched opinion. I took a survey at the DA head offices and everyone said so, so you know it's true.

He rose to prominence under the most famous South African *sgebenga* of all time, Jacob Zuma. Just a few years ago, he was the president of the ANC Youth League and now he's all like 'pay back the money'. I know, right!

He got into a big fight with Jacob, or something like that. They were frenemies but now they're real enemies. This is like when I was in varsity and my ex-friend Megan told everyone my real name when I specifically asked her not to and she said I'm not woke. That would mean I'm asleep, Megan! And I couldn't be writing this if I'm asleep. Think about it!

Anyway, now we're not friends and she owes me R7 000 from our Tashas dinners, I counted. And she won't pay back the money. This is exactly what happened with JZ and Julius, so I get it.

Julius only had a matric until, like, yesterday when he clearly bought his degree. You can tell that because he can barely speak English. I speak English very well. All the white people I meet compliment me on it and it's such an amazing feeling to know that they recognise that in me as I'm trying really hard.

You'll recognise Julius as the dude who is always shouting in Parliament. He's always saying 'point of order' really loudly and interrupting people. He never even says 'excuse me'. How can you trust someone who doesn't have manners?

And he also wants to nationalise everything, including farms! My friends' parents and grand- parents worked really hard to get those farms in the colonial and/or apartheid days. They were really polite about it. They asked people to please move out so they could make food for us. That's really cool because otherwise we wouldn't have any food.

● ● ● ● ● ● ● ● ● ●
Black People don't know how to farm
● ● ● ● ● ● ● ● ● ●

Black people don't know how to farm. I mean, they do the labour and know the lay of the land but white people are the ones who come up with the ideas. So, without a boss, black people will only be standing there doing crimes or whatever.

Malema is also such a reverse racist. He sings about killing the boers! I mean, if a white person were to do that, everyone would be up in arms, but nooo, there are no consequences for Malema because this country protects blacks.

In conclusion, he's the worst.

Floyd Shivambu: Now don't be fooled, old Shivambs is another Julius. His brother, Brian (they really trick you with these good old-fashioned Caucasian names, don't they?) was part of the now-defunct VBS Bank.

I have to mention that I would never trust a bank that was started in Limpopo. Venda people are the darkest and the mistrust level of a black person is directly proportionate to how much melanin he or she has. Anyway, those VBS people stole a whole lot of money, or was it diamonds or cars? I'm not really sure because the news is *so* boring, LOL.

But I know that it was bad because the DA was really vocal about it. And we are only vocal about things that *really* matter, like colonialism.

Anyway, Shivambu was also part of the ANC. There's not much more to say. This is someone who scares me.

Dali Mpofu: He defended Patricia de Lille so he's the worst of them all. He literally betrayed Helen, who actually liked him. There is nothing more to say. He's dead to me.

Mbuyiseni Ndlozi: He's actually cute for a black guy. He's the only decent one there, really. It's a pity the DA didn't get him sooner: he'd make a great puppet leader because even the blacks like him. Don't get it twisted, though, I'm still strictly vanilla – but ja, a decent oke.

The one good thing they can stand on is that they all have degrees, unlike so many of those ANC politicians, but that's about all that is commendable about them. The bad thing is that, if they get into power, the last remaining white people will move back to Europe and then it's literal dark times for this country. That's not okay.

ANC

Speaking of the ANC (😒), this is by far the most corrupt party that has ever led South Africa! Even more so than the National Party. Because even though apartheid was bad, it wasn't as bad as Nkandla! Like, Jacob really let Mandela down. This is not what he meant when he made the famous 'I Have a Dream' speech upon his release from jail in, like, the olden days.

And my reverse-racist dad always says that the NP was even more corrupt but I'm, like, where's the evidence? Okay, so black people weren't allowed to move freely and they were arrested but that was only the *sgebengas* (Mandela was more of a 'wrong place, wrong time' kind of person and that's why De Klerk forgave him and he became a hero; also, he created the term 'rainbow nation').

Cyril Ramaphosa: Cyril is one of the good ones. We white people and white-adjacents all celebrated when he became president. This is because he took walks on the promenade and he was already rich, which means he won't steal white people's stolen land.

All the black people are complaining that petrol keeps going up and they want to blame good ol' Cyril for it but maybe if they didn't *tshontsha* cars and actually worked hard for once, they'd be able to afford it.

Cyril also has a game farm and it's so beautiful. And he is Patrice Motsepe's brother-in-law so that's more reason to trust him. Patrice is really one of the very best blacks. He's brought Beyoncé to South Africa, so #thinkaboutit.

Malusi Gigaba: While Malusi is not *that* important in the greater scheme of things he is the personification of this party so I'll touch on him.

Firstly, he is verrry dark, guys. And secondly, his eyes are verrrry close together, like a predator in the wild. These two things alone tell you everything you need to know. Also, he is friends with the Guptas and that already spells t-r-o-u-b-l-e.

Not-so-fun fact: his phone password is 000000 like Kanye's and that's how everyone always knows his secrets. For someone nick-named Gigabyte, he doesn't know much about technology.

● ● ● ● ● ● ● ● ● ●
$000000 =$
Gigaba's
password
● ● ● ● ● ● ● ● ● ●

Jacob Zuma: Old Zoom Zoom away (you see, more puns!) may be 'retired' but we're not taking our eyes off that one. A *sgeb* is forever plotting. Even today, he is always dancing and singing. Only if you have something to hide do you sing and dance *that* much. It's a distraction technique to blind the black people into thinking he is nice and friendly like the Teletubbies. But he's more like the Gremlins.

Zuma even dropped out of school, like, in kindergarten so how do you trust someone who draws pictures and can only count to eleventy? And he is always laughing. He's laughing at us. I know it.

The reason why Zuma is so bad is because he let the Gupta and those Watsons from Bosasa buy South Africa. I didn't even know our country was for sale or I would've asked my dad to buy it for me for my birthday. We're rich, so he can afford it.

Anyway, unlike the DA, the cANCer sponsors are not white. This means they are dangerous and only want to enrich other non-white people. This is not good. Can you imagine a world with white helpers and black bosses? Yikes. Chaos!

In short, there is nothing good about the cANCer. Nothing at all. Everything is bad. Well, excluding Uncle Cyril, of course, but he's not enough to save the party.

Democratic Alliance

White helpers and black bosses = Chaos in the world

Undoubtedly, and without bias, the best party South Africa has ever had is the DA. The party was started before I was born and back then it was called the Democratic Party. The first leader I became aware of was Tony Leon, may his mercy endure forever.

This was the party that brought apartheid to an end. Everyone in the DA says they voted 'For' in the 1992 whites-only referendum. Yes, if it wasn't for the freedom fighters and finger-waggers, there would still be all those evil laws.

None of the white people who support the DA ever supported apartheid . . . and if they did, they obviously had their reasons. At least they are woke enough to lie about it now because when you know better, you do better.

This is the only party in which the rainbow nation ideals still stand strong. It's not BEE compliant because BEE is a ruse to get white people to leave the country and that's called reverse apartheid.

Helen Zille: Her full title within the party is 'Eternal Leader and Natural Blonde Goddess Supreme. The One Who Single-handedly Fought for Our Freedom and for the Right to Compliment Colonialism, Helen Gogo Zille'. Helen is a role model because she went right up to the apartheid government and asked to speak to the manager; when she went through, they knew it was over scadovers.

A while ago she was confronted by some controversy due to a few ungrateful blacks who disagreed with her opinions about colonialism. Look, the fact of the matter is that, before Jan van Riebeeck came and liberated the savage Africans, they were hunting and gathering.

Jan van Riebeeck: liberator of savage Africans On his boat he brought Kumon maths, English tutors and tailors to make cute clothes for everyone. We literally wouldn't have maths if not for the white people who kindly bought it from Egypt, which technically is in Africa but whatever. We are grateful.

We would still be running around the jungle if not for that. And yes 'blah blah atrocities', but guys, would you rather not have had apartheid and slavery but still be living in the jungle? I mean, technically there is no jungle here, and globalisation would have brought all the advancements, some of which were thanks to Africans anyway, but that's not the point.

I digress. Helen speaks isiXhosa, which she learnt from *Clicking For Dummies*, and she hugs black babies and stirs pots in the township. Your fave could never!

Mmusi Maimane: Mmusi took over from that ungrateful Lindiwe. People always ask where he came from with, like, three years' experience but hello, you can get a degree in three years (which he did at the University of Quota, majoring in Tokenism). Obviously, quota systems only work if they benefit ~~white people~~ *everyone*.

When Lindiwe decided to turn on the DA after everything Helen did for her – sorry, I'm still upset – Mmusi was voted most likely to appeal to black voters who can't see what's going on and obviously white voters coz he speaks so well and he has a beautiful pearly-white wife.

Mmusi is the leader. But he's obvs not the *leader* leader. Because that will always be Helen. He is a good leader-ish, though, and a great mouthpiece. Helen says that is what they call loyal blacks. I can't wait to be a mouthpiece.

The other people like Belinda Bozzoli, Natasha Mazzone and many more make the DA feel like family. Well, the family that gives you the other crockery. But I prefer having my own crockery anyway because #germaphobe.

This is the only party that looks after the rights of ~~white people~~ *everyone* so well. It only makes sense that you would leave whichever third-grade party you have invested in and join the DA today!

I hope my political wisdom and thorough research (some of which will be published in my master's thesis with the working title *Die Real Stem: DA ambitions and glory from the beginning until forever*) really makes you think about the party you associate with.

Don't vote for the ANC and then complain when they take

your money. And stop asking when the DA will fix Khaye-litsha and the inequality in Cape Town and focus on the good – the Atlantic Seaboard is gorgeous and when you're there it feels like you're in Europe.

This is not my opinion . . . it's fact, guys. Wikipedia it – you know Wikipedia is the most factual and honest source on the internet. Everything else is fake news (except, of course, the DA website).

11
Hosting 101

Being the unofficial DA mascot is not always easy. For one thing, I am constantly hosting dinners and events in an effort to get more people to vote for the party.

You see, I am part of the party planning committee. Again, this is on an unofficial basis but I do enjoy getting fellow enthusiasts together to talk about the future of this country and how we can make it look like the past again.

This chapter will help you elevate your social status from white to white supreme by teaching you how to host the perfect Caucasian shindig. I would have said 'party', but that is how black people let things get out of control. People must know they are attending a shindig, or soiree, so that they know to enter with trepidation in full understanding that it will start and finish on time.

Shindig
A function which starts and ends on time

Once you have acquired this skill, your transformation and assimilation process will be complete and you will finally be seen as one of them. At this point, you will have to say goodbye to your entire family. They will no longer be a part of your life. And that is okay. If this were easy, everyone would have been able to live the life of white privilege. But it is not, and that is why this life is reserved for those of us who want it badly enough.

Time

Black people do not know this thing, because they have a terrible relationship with clocks. It goes back to Robben Island where they never had clocks so they did not learn how to tell

African time

Black people are notoriously late for *everything*

the time and consequently could not pass that knowledge on to later generations.

As a result of this, black people are notoriously late for everything. *Everything.* So much so that the term 'African time' has been coined. It is easily the most frustrating thing from my past life, before I had moved on and declared myself transracial (same as Rachel Dolezal but better coz my declaration is the right way around).

However, in this world of hosting, on the Tropic of Caucasity time is extremely important. It is of the essence, even. For this reason, and a whole host of others, I felt I never really belonged in my race and I wanted to disassociate from them.

A great soiree starts at 11 am. This is because you want people to have eaten their own breakfast so that they are not starving by the time they get to you. Soirees are for networking and ooh-ing and aah-ing. Not for eating. What are we? Darkies? LOL, well, we're trying not to be.

The soiree will progress into a shindig at about 3 pm. This is when enough drinks have flowed for the guests to be feeling like hitting the line dance. 'Cotton-Eyed Joe' is perfect to get the party started! Things will need to wind down by late afternoon (so just an hour for dancing, then everyone will leave your house by 5 pm). It is magical the swiftness white people adopt when they need to leave a house. Unlike the ingrates who come and turn your house into Taboo or whatever.

Food

Any great hostess knows that the focus of a party can never be the food, but that the food does play a part in whether you come across as poor or not. The worst thing you can do is serve meat. This is not a carnival . . . there is no reason to be walking around holding meat, unless it is a corndog in a 1990s romcom.

The most popular kind of food for the perfect white soiree is the perfectly crafted and decrusted cucumber sandwich. All your guests are vegan-adjacent, so only a little bit of butter – you do not want them to notice, but that bread can be so dry without it and become a choking hazard.

DO NOT
Take a bite and a sip at the same time. It is *uncouth.*

Black people take a bite and sip at the same time. It is uncouth, but it is effective. Perhaps that's what I miss the most about my old life. WAIT! Sorry. Oh my goodness. What a strange thing to say. I do not miss anything about my old life.

Another great type of beloved Caucasian food is a cherry tomato and vheese (vegan cheese) cube on a toothpick. The novelty of eating from a tiny toothpick never gets old at these things. What an eclectic way to bring some fun into your home. There is a whole cookbook on toothpick delicacies made by super-white chef Jamie Oliver. He even has some meat varieties for when your guests party into the night (like if it is a wedding).

If there is someone who is really hungry, firstly, shoot them a look because it is really rude to be hungry in someone else's house. Also, feed them quinoa balls. These are like meatballs without the flavour or deliciousness or joy.

I found a hummus recipe that would make your mouth water; mine is watering now! It uses the very best chickpeas grown locally right here on the Line of Caucus, harvested, picked and finally crushed by the resentment of an unheard workforce. I served it at my latest event and I even heard someone say, 'That tastes nice.' Coming from a more staid crowd, this could not have been a better compliment!

Décor

I once was looking for a European channel for my friends on my TV and we stumbled upon a documentary that my helper loves to watch – *Our Perfect Wedding*. I could only watch it for two seconds before I started to feel shame and embarrassment. My friends looked at me for the first time like they *could* see colour and I started to physically feel my melanin. Gross.

I was really mad at my mom because I asked her for the premium white package where you only get European and Afrikaans channels. I had sort of been exposed. I am exceptionally good at using the word 'anyway!' to get people to move along swiftly.

Why am I bringing up this show? Because every week someone puts décor on their wish list for creating the perfect wedding and every week it is *no bueno* (or so I have been told). The planner is never on time and the décor part of the wish list goes to shit. Again, this is what I've heard, not watched.

The other problem is that black people love a tent. Tents are quite ghetto. Marquees are more refined. An adult black who is, let's say, thirty years old has, on average, been to twenty celebrations and funerals inside a tent. This is why they are obsessed with tents – nostalgia and a current, never-ending trend.

Tents
Loved by
black people

Marquees
More refined

They also always insist on draping. A tablecloth, a napkin, someone's dress . . . if it can be draped, it will be. And lastly, they love thrones. Yes, it is important to be the centre of attention at your party, but you want your dress and dancing to catch that attention. Not a ghetto throne.

Oh and before I forget, they also always incorporate a lace food cover, which my reverse-racist grandmother uses all the time.

If you want to have amazing décor at your soiree, there are a few things to remember: always have a clock as the focal point of the room so that when you clear your throat and force them to look up, they will instantly see that it is time to get the exodus going from the host house. The tablecloths have got to be made of 10 000 thread count Egyptian cotton. If it is anything less than that, you might as well call it your farewell party because you can kiss white high society goodbye. If it is a dinner party, each table setting should have a name so that you can separate the liberals from the better people. Ugh. You do not want to be talking about how there are too many Chinese people in South Africa and their government is taking over right next to a hippie who believes in BEE or something.

Everything about the setup should be white: linens, flowers, bottles of champagne and, of course, guests. White is clean, white is rich, white is elegant, white is power, white is right.

And as part of the décor, there should be a station for everyone to drop their kids and dogs off. They all play in one pen since they all mess themselves. You get a number and you can collect the corresponding dog or baby when you leave. There will be more than enough nannies and au pairs to look after them.

• • • • • • • • • • • • • •

WHITE

White is clean
White is rich
White is elegant
White is power
White is right

• • • • • • • • • • • • •

Drinks

The perfect drink for a host to serve her friends is champagne. But, like, the expensive and authentic type. Not the local sparkling wine. Not because it does not taste nice. It does. But remember, the only point of hosting is to show your friends and frenemies that you are richer than them and have resources, like toothpicks and food, to waste.

There are some cocktails you probably have not heard of but which are high up on the list of desired drinks. You need to get familiar with them if you want to assimilate well. The one you might know is a White Russian. The name is pretty self-explanatory.

Other cocktails are:

- Sex on the Whites-only Beach
- Long Island Plantation Iced Tea
- White Lady
- Old-fashioned Lynching
- Negroni (LOL, just kidding!)

All these drinks come in a virgin version for if you bring your kids. And some Oros for their nannies. Trust me, they love Oros just as much as we love our cocktails!

Table settings

Now, you do not want to come off as being too ostentatious, but again, people must envy you and think you are a bright example of white wealth, regardless of the race you started out as.

The first thing you need are place cards. White people do not like to sit down unless they are told where to sit. This is also just basic manners. But remember who is friends with who and who hates who because where you put them could make the difference between your getting your race card stamped or not!

Remember, 2019 is about bohemian style. It follows on from the past ten years that were also all bohemian because we do not enjoy change. After all, that is the only reason apartheid lasted so long. Like, they knew it was bad but they are creatures of comfort, you know? To create your bohemian look, you are going to want to buy plenty of things that make it look like you live outside but in a rich way. Think fairy lights, lanterns for the candles, random tree trunks and mason jars, which, if you go to the right store, should set you back by R8 000.

The food budget is limited, with the only costs being flying the cucumbers in from the Queen's garden in London, so you have space and money to play around with here. The table is just there so you can reach the cucumber better and fake-smile at that bitch, Patricia, who copied your hibiscus idea and stole your shine.

Music

As previously stated, this is not some disco for your friends to have a wild time at. This is a sophisticated Caucesque soiree. So, when choosing your DJ, go the route of classic old-school music from such famous racists as Elvis. Ah, the good old days of the front of the bus being a privilege. What a time.

You want the music to play on vinyl so that it seems like it is playing both here and far away. So far away that you are back in high school and the only Thembi there is, is the one who cleans. And even she can't deny the beauty of the music of that time.

Guest list

The people you invite will truly make or break your gathering. This is because there are popular people, and there are the people who will sink you into social oblivion.

There is no hard and fast rule that says you can't invite a black person. But the ratio always has to make the white women feel comfortable and not need to have more than one conversation with Thandi from the office. Oh yes, it is better if she is a colleague – they'll understand better why she is there.

You might be thinking, *But won't they see I'm black if I invite black friends?* No. If you are hosting an event, it means you are already three-quarters of the way into the full transformation process. At this point, when they say they do not see colour, they will be talking about your translucent skin, post-bleach.

You also want to invite people from the country club you wish to be a part of. Then they can enjoy your hospitality and go speak to their husbands on your behalf to let you in.

Conversation topics

You may think that soiree conversation is organic, something that just happens because people connect. Oh, you silly fool! Everything has to be guided and suggested because, as women, we do not want the bother of thinking too hard about the world, otherwise we might get sad.

I bet you are wondering how on earth you can guide conversation when you can't be everywhere at once. Well, we Caucasian women call it coding. You will put various objects and pictures around the room in the conversation zones so that people bounce off that. For extra help in case things get really tough, each guest will receive a pack of key cards with a few ideas for conversation topics.

You should come up with your own key cards, because each party and group is different. Just to get you started, here are a few of the most popular conversation topics:

- The crime is getting out of hand, this country is going to the dogs! I am moving to . . .
- No, come on man, it has been twenty-five years. They must get over it.' (This only applies to apartheid. Not the Holocaust or 9/11 or World War I.)
- 'Ever since I started juicing . . .'
- 'No, my husband works at . . . We never get free time, but we do love our Decembers in . . .'
- 'No man, why can't they see how corrupt the ANC is? Really can't believe they invented corruption!'
- 'That Muzi Maimunni is such a non-threatening black. And that makes him a great future leader. He has a white wife, you know.'

They must get over it

The crime is getting out of hand.

That Muzi Maimunni is such a non-threatening black.

- 'So now we have a quota rugby captain. Oh, he is very good? One of the best? Yes, but still. These people and handouts.'
- 'I'm not being racist but . . .' (Then go wild. You have excused yourself so you can be as racist as you want – have fun with it.)

The last thing to take note of in order to be the perfect host is . . .

Service staff

You will never be able to host any sort of party without a great staff at your service. This not only includes your current maid and/or butler – you will need to ask them to invite their friends to come and help as well. Failing that, you can hire a team with the help of your event coordinator.

You need to ensure that you buy uniforms for them because you do not want people to think that you would have that many black people in your house voluntarily. You will need at least two days before the event for proper training. Imagine the embarrassment of people getting served from the left instead of the right!

The service staff must become invisible, almost as if you have magical trays that are floating by themselves in the air. Again, your guests' inability to see colour will help here.

The staff must not talk too loudly. That would be a nightmare. They must feel slightly on edge – as if they know you could bring slavery back at any minute – but not angry so that they would turn around and rob you.

Add an extra R5 to their fee and get them to entertain the guests with a song or two. When I go to game reserves, my favourite thing is to see the exploited staff sing for my white delight.

Please take photos of your next soiree and tag me in them so I can follow your progress and cheer you on from a distance. I will also be able to give notes for improvement, just in case I see something out of place like one too many blacks . . . or meat platters. Enjoy!

PS Despite my having hosted many a soiree, nothing seems to get the DA to take me more seriously. Nothing I do actually seems to convince anyone higher up to make me a member of staff. That's A-okay, though; I smile through the pain and tell myself I do it because I believe in the party. It is not for me to question why, when I have worked my ass off for years and never deviated from the agreed-upon rules. Just the other day, Phumzile and Mmusi started replying to tweets in isi-Vernac! That is rule number two in the Handbook for Avoiding Harvard (rule number one is Helen is the *leader* leader and shall therefore face no consequences for any actions – and that is only right).

Oh gosh, I apologise for this rant! But rather write an angry e-mail and never press send than let them find out how frustrated you are by your lack of real progress.

12

#VayCay

Holidaying, like every other activity you can think of in South Africa, is split along the racial divide. And that's a good thing. You have holidays for black people (these are holidays you must never admit to having gone on) and then you have proper holidays to further the image you are working on so hard.

To survive this shithole, you need to do everything in your power to ascend to whiteness in all its glory. That includes picking the right kind of holiday. Remember, this is the whole point of why I am writing this book – I want to show you how to live a better life, so you not only survive but thrive.

I am a native Joburger (well, I have traced my ancestry to Ireland – I did the test with my friend Siobhan O'Shaughnessy and the doctor did seem a little confused but I *feel* Irish). But Gauteng will not be included, because I do not holiday here: I live here and work here and Caucus here. There are also other places I won't include because they don't matter. My main focus is the top places that separate the haves (melanin) from the have-nots (melanin).

The first thing to note is that black people mainly go on

holiday over certain holiday periods. That is, Christmas, Easter and their own holidays like the Durban July. So, the best time for you to go to the Caucasian hubs is over these periods. Then you won't have to bear witness to their descending in the thousands on the beaches we love and keep clean all year round. It really makes you miss those good old days of the *slegs blankes* (whites only) beaches. Although even then the transracial community should've been welcomed, because we are the good ones, you guys. I mean, we do not collect seawater, we do not slaughter sheep on the beaches, and we do not go in groups of more than five. We also have swimming costumes, unlike them in their tights and T-shirts. You can distinguish them from us easily, as they will have a plastic bag over their heads for protection from the *manzi* (water). And do not ask me why they collect the water because I have no idea. It's not something I have ever done, I promise.

Right, so when you start to plan your trip there are a few things to remember. The first is that black people hate the cold. Anthropologically speaking, the melanin in their skin attracts the cold and they feel it more strongly than we do. In general, any kind of winter getaway is perfect because black people are mostly hibernating. I've never thought about it before, but black people are the bears of human beings. The bears and the monkeys, actually.

> **Black people**
> The bears and monkeys of human beings

The second is that black people are last-minute bookers and lazy vacationers . . . and as such, they usually go on the same type of low-class holiday. Their patterns are usually easy to spot, so just read more on www.WWBD.CIDWI.co.za (what would blacks do coz I don't want it) to stay ahead of the curve and avoid their hotspots.

I will break my holidaying guide down by the most popular provinces to vacation in and the cities that usually serve black people best, as well as the peak times for the different races to vacation there. The black side may look tempting at times, because for all their blackness these people are a fun lot. Fight temptation and align yourself with the holidays of Caucasity.

KWAZULU-NATAL

The most popular province for Joburgers to vacation in is undoubtedly KZN. This is for both whites and blacks (I have never studied the Indian people on holiday in great depth, but I assume it's a really popular province for them too since they will not leave it, LOLz).

But not all of KwaZulu-Natal is the right KwaZulu-Natal. In fact, one could even separate it into KwaZulu for you-know-who and Natal for us British and British-aspirant folk.

Before you book your trip, establish when the most congested time of year is. There are three peak seasons – commonly referred to as the blackpocalypses – to avoid:

* Christmas/New Year and Easter. This time is shared with friends and family. Despite it being a terribly over-

crowded time, it is not as rowdy as one would think. Avoid driving anywhere near the N3 around these times because the traffic is so bothersome. And to think, there isn't even a highway manager to complain to about your time being wasted. So, fly. But not to Durban . . .

Black-pocalypses
Peak seasons

- During the Durban July. This is when husbands leave their wives at home and travel with a much younger and more enthusiastic but less-well-trained girlfriend. The hotel bar becomes a tavern, and the rooms and villas mini Taboo nightclubs.

The July gets rowdy, let me tell you. It's a cacophony of music and their naturally loud voices. You might think I am 'othering' myself here, but keep in mind that I asserted long ago that I was in fact transracial and on my journey to enlightenment. My white friends and their parents compliment me all the time that I am not like The Others and tell me my hard work is being acknowledged. I am well on my way 😊.

Now to figure out where (not) to go. The most popular areas for the darker folk are:

Zimbali

This is by far the most popular place for the rich ones and everyone in the blesser–blessee community. You know, once they decide that a place is the new 'it' spot, they flock to it like flies to hungry children.

If you are a homeowner there, ummm what are you waiting for? Sell your place with immediate effect and get a home in a more suitable location. One away from the portable speakers and 'a yo yo yohs' that fill the night sky during peak times. Even the golf course does not discriminate. Unfortunately, you will see many an inflated BEE tummy trying to sink balls but holding the club like an *iklwa* (or assegai, as we would better know it).

The place is super beautiful and makes for amazing Instagram photos, so it really is a pity that it has been overrun with *sgebenga* types. Now, they can't swim, of course, but Lord knows they will swarm to the pool and beach areas, once again to take more snaps. Last time I was there, a girl's wig fell off and she clogged the entire pool, which had to be drained. This meant a whole twenty-four hours of no swimming.

Hayikhona, wena!

Another area they have expropriated without compensating is Umhlanga ('Uhmshlanga', phonetically). Once-esteemed hotels like the Beverly Hills and The Oyster Box and the newly developed The Pearls have been taken over by them.

Do not even get me started on Umhlanga Ridge as a residential area, nicknamed the border between the Soweto and Lenasia of Umhlanga by my friend Meg's dad because of the people who live there. But if you focus on what I have written in this chapter, you will know that, outside of peak times, you will find times when the black people have dispersed (probably to go rob more people to save up for the next takeover).

On the opposite side of the spectrum, we have white-people holidays – the 'bougie' to Zimbali's 'bad'.

Ballito and Umdloti

You would think that, because of its proximity to Zimbali, you would run into problems here. Lo and behold, the opposite could not be truer.

It's the moment (place, in this instance) in *The Lion King* where the light touches the ground. The darkness that is Zimbali and its hyenas can be seen in the distance, but is far enough away that you could be in two different provinces. Also, when they go to Gateway for their shopping needs, you can sneak into Ballito Lifestyle Centre for all your green juice ingredients and to buy a sneaky chai latte to calm your nerves.

Now, with regards to Umdloti (pronounced Uhmshloti), when I was first told about this area as a potential vacation spot, my jaw almost shattered on the floor. I mean, why would a place with such an African name – and such a tongue-twister – appeal to the great white masses? Then I learnt about Durban's bad habit of naming everything in isiZulu. After a riot broke out about the English names, no doubt. You should see the street names: it's like the who's who of the Rivonia Treason Trial but not even the famous ones like Mandela.

Contrary to its name, Umdloti is heavenly white. The only people of colour I've ever interacted with are staff and those who have somehow tricked the mâitre d' with false accents and booked a table at one of the beachfront spots. (They may actually be transracial, now that I think about it. This is not something people speak about proudly because of the back-lash and teasing, so I can't actually assume that they are not one of us. Allow me to retract that judgemental statement, but only that one.)

The best time for a holiday here is literally any time of the year except the three major blackpocalypses – although you could get away with Ballito during those times because it's still pretty safe. They go to South Beach and Umhlanga over the peak season, so avoid these, which you would anyway, because South Beach, you guys. It's *no bueno*.

WESTERN CAPE

Another favourite for rich *sgebengas* and the pure race alike. Different season, different reasons, but the result is the same.

Cape Town

They have discovered it and they are coming in thick and fast. I spent my Easter holiday in Cape Town and even when I was trying to get away to the *binneland* to sip some slave-labour, 'git offa my propertee', White Monopoly Capital, Stein-hoff-flavoured grapes, there they were, staring at me with that hunter gaze.

I could not escape them that entire weekend. But then again, it was the Two Oceans Marathon and if there is one thing they love to do, it's run. It is because all they do all day is run, so they have an unfair advantage. They run to the taxis, run from the police, run from their fatherhood responsibilities, run their mouths, etc. You see, running all day. So anyway,

Blacks love to run, they

- run to the taxis
- run from the police
- run from their fatherhood responsibilites
- run their mouths
- run, run, run

they come by the taxiload to compete in the Two Oceans and so the city is like a candy bar left on the grass on a summer's day.

They even know Camps Bay, guys. I almost choked on my foie gras. A little anecdote (and this is a true story) for reference. A few years ago, before I began my transition to Caucasity, I went to lunch in Camps Bay with my friends, at one of the popular spots that I shall not name because it is besides the point. Anyway, at about 5 pm. the taxis loaded up and started heading back to the townships. Now, Cape Town might not have apartheid legally but this is one city that has really kept that pass laws/Group Areas Act vibe going well into the twenty-first century. I'm proud, actually, and in awe.

But wait, where was I? As the last taxis were loading up someone whom I can only assume was the manager came over and dropped our bill on the table. When we enquired what the hell was going on, since we were still sipping on our cocktails, he explained that he did not want us to miss our transport and be stranded in Camps Bay.

I was baffled; how could people be so stupid to have spent as much as we had on dinner and drinks, not to have made solid plans to get home? So all of this is just to express my

— 170 —

surprise at how easy it seems to navigate that space these days. Twitter says otherwise, but I saw them with my own eyes.

We all know the tragic story of Clifton Beach, so I don't even need to go there. The place went from peacefully AWB to EFF way too quickly. Is it such a bad thing for people not to want black people on their public beaches? Is it so awful to hanker back to the times of apartheid and wish nothing had changed? I mean, surely you understand we just do not want to feel threatened. That is all. But then you want the Anglo-Zulu War Part Two and go around stabbing things, which proves our point in the first place.

It took so long to clean the sand, you guys. Maids were sent with buckets and mops for two weeks until it was all done. I have not returned to the scene of the crime, neither have I been able to eat lamb or mutton again. This senseless murder was bigger than any 'police brutality' (read: crime prevention) in America. It was an innocent animal! Much like the rhino, but again, I digress.

Don't go to Clifton from Christmas Eve until a week into the new year. We can no longer fight them being on the beaches but that doesn't mean we have to watch them.

Winelands/Hout Bay/Knysna/George/Plett/Wilderness/Simon's Town

Basically everywhere else in the Western Cape, except the rudimentary city centre of Cape Town, is where you can enjoy the sights and sounds of the quieter and whiter Cape coastline. These towns see about 1,4 black families a year on average, so really they are the right places to visit.

I think of these towns and I think, 'Ahh, sweet segregation'. Places like this are throwback Thursdays of note, if the throwback Thursday photo was of a whites-only bench or a train carrying blacks back to their homeland after sunset. They disappear into the night, only to return the next morning with a roasty cuppa.

The Garden Route should be called the Lily Route because it's white, it's right and it's sooo pretty! I've also never seen a black lily. Most of the guesthouses in these places would sooner shut down or burn themselves down than have a black guest. I know this because of my experience in my former life.

I think this is another reason to consider living by transracial principles, even if you refuse to change. Life is simply easier when you assimilate. You are not a thirty-year-old in a Broadway chorus line . . . you do not need to stand out or make a *scene*.

Things to enjoy along the Western Cape coastline are such Caucasian-inspired activities like jam-making and buying souvenirs. The flora out there is just spectacular and mostly indigenous – and this is a sentence that no black has ever uttered in their lives.

EASTERN CAPE

This is the one province where you never ever have to worry. Holidays here are so separate they might as well be a 1950s bus. Although this province does not quite offer the sophisticated but overt racism of the wondrous Western Cape, the people themselves are so divided it's impossible to get it wrong.

Umtata/Port Elizabeth/East London

Here is the thing about black holidays in the Eastern Cape. Unlike the other provinces and cities mentioned above, in terms of black people, this province seems to receive only 'homecoming' visitors or wedding attendees. The *lalis* are here as well. Not sure in which direction because, eek! I would rather die.

The homecoming visitors would most likely be of the Xhosa tribe. My anthropology project was on Nelson Mandela and he was one, so by deduction I can say they are a valiant people, a peaceful people, and they have a weirdly funny accent.

There's nothing more to say here. They call everyone *mchana* which is literally derived from the slang (howzit) 'my china' or 'hello friend, I mean you no harm'. Learn that, and you will be good to go should you need to drive through an Eastern Cape town to get to one of the pot-of-gold white towns.

St Francis Bay/Kenton-on-Sea/Port St Johns/Jeffrey's Bay . . . all the bays, really

These are the treasure troves of white vacation towns. The towns that nobody knows and hardly anyone speaks about (I mean, in black circles).

They are kind of like the Loch Ness Monster to them, or the *tokoloshe*, if you will. You are convinced they exist, but you have never seen them and you do not know anyone who has, either. Among white people, this is a closely guarded secret.

There are very few hotels in the towns – mostly homes owned by your schoolmates' parents. This is why no one new gets in without proper discussion with and agreement from the Grand Wizards of the East. This is what they are affectionately known as, because they are magical.

Here, people walk like they are listening to 'Blue Suede Shoes' all the time: there is a spring in their step and they have a carefree aura that says, 'I'm safe here.' In the words of the immortal Adam Catzavelos, there is 'not a k****r in sight!'

An honourable mention goes to The Bush. If you want to see many black people, keep it basic with your Mpumalangas and Limpopos. Yikes!

But if you want that *Jock of the Bushveld* vibe where the only black face you will see is the one painted on Leon Schuster, head across the border to the national parks in Botswana, Namibia or Zambia. It's white guests only, I promise. The rest are only there to work.

Here's an even better tip. For a proper blacks-free holiday, there's always an overseas trip. Think Europe! Europe! Europe! But not the countries with scary immigration numbers like France or the United Kingdom. No, you want proper European, like the night before the first ships sailed for the colonies. Head to Russia, Ukraine or the Nordic region. Bliss!

And if you want racism served medium-well, head to the good ol' US of A. They have rebranded and are back with a bang! Serving racism à la carte – you even get to choose your preferred version.

Now, happy holidaying!

Acknowledgements

To my parents (all four of you), thank you for always supporting me and allowing me to chase my dream even when you didn't quite understand it. You understood me, and that is all a creative like me needs. I love you.

To my family and friends, you applaud every achievement, big or small, and always make sure I go out into the world with confidence, knowing I am loved. You have no idea how important that is in this crazy world I am now thrust into. Thank you.

To my boyfriend, thank you for always having a back rub or a drink waiting after hours of me typing and allowing me to hibernate when the going got tough. For always being a cheerleader and shoulder to cry on. I love you.

To my crazy aunties, your daughters are forces in the world because we had phenomenal role models in you. Thank you for always cheering us on so hard and for being hilariously crazy. I got it from you.

To the team at Jonathan Ball Publishers, thank you for working tirelessly to make my dreams come true. Being a published author was something I thought would happen much later. So thank you for taking a chance on me and bringing my crazy to life.

An extra thank you to my momager – you always make sure the whole world knows what to tune into. You always pick me up on lower days when the negativity gets overwhelming. And you are such a spiritual fountain for me to drink from that I always know I'm protected. You have given up a lot for me to do this. I am eternally grateful.

CPSIA information can be obtained
at www.ICGtesting.com
Printed in the USA
BVHW041403040919
557561BV00012B/237/P